# Top Spee

# CARS

Pagani Huayra BC

Created and produced by:
Green Android Ltd
49 Beaumont Court, Upper Clapton Road,
London E5 8BG, United Kingdom
www.greenandroid.co.uk

ISBN 978-1-912188-03-1

Copyright © Green Android Ltd 2017

Despite extensive research of current sources, performance and economy figures for cars can vary due to inconsistency and local variables in testing methods. Sometimes, figures are estimates or simply not available.

**Picture credits**
FC: Bugatti. **p1** (tl) Aston Martin Lagonda; (tr) Dodge; (bl) Mercedes-Benz (Daimler AG); (br) Nissan Motor Co. **p2–3** Pagani Automobili SpA. **p4–5** Spyker NV. **p6–7** Mercedes-Benz (Daimler AG). **p8–9** Mini (BMW). **p18–19** Mercedes-Benz (Daimler AG). **p30–31** BMW. **p42–43** BAC. **p52–53** Mercedes-Benz (Daimler AG). **p66–67** Alfa Romeo (FCA). **p82–83** Jaguar Land Rover. **p96–97** Dodge (FCA). **p110–111** Ferrari SpA.

All remaining pictures are copyright of the relevant model's motor manufacturer: Alfa Romeo (FCA), Abarth & C SpA (FCA), Ariel Motor Co, Aston Martin Lagonda Ltd, Automobili Lamborghini SpA, Audi AG and UK, BAC (Briggs Automotive Co), Bentley Motors Ltd, BMW AG and UK, Bugatti, Cadillac, Caparo plc, Caterham Cars, Chevrolet, Dodge (FCA), Elemental Motor Co Ltd, Ferrari SpA, Fiat Automobiles (FCA), Ford Motor Co, GM (General Motors), Hennessey Performance Engineering, Holden Australia, Honda Motor Co, ItalDesign Giugiaro SpA, Jaguar Land Rover, Jeep (FCA), Koenigsegg Automotive AB, KTM AG, Lexus, Lotus Group, Maserati SpA (FCA), Mazda Motor Corp, McLaren Automotive, Mercedes-Benz (Daimler AG), Mini (BMW), Morgan Motor Co, NIO, Nissan Motor Co Ltd, Pagani Automobili SpA, Peugeot/Group PSA, Porsche AG and UK, Opel Automobile GmgH, Radical Sportscars, Groupe Renault, Rolls-Royce Motor Cars (BMW), Scuderia Cameron Glickenhaus LLC, Seat SA, smart Automobile (Daimler AG), Spyker NV, TechRules, Tesla Inc, Vanda Electrics Pte Ltd, Vauxhall Motors UK, Volkswagen Group, Volvo Car Corporation and Zenvo Automotive AS.

Printed and bound in Malaysia, November 2017

# Top Speed

# CARS

## 100 EXTREME MACHINES

Small aileron and low-drag air inlet on the Spyker C8 Preliator supercar.

# Contents

It was three-time drivers' world champion, Sir Jackie Stewart, who coined the name 'Green Hell' for the Nordschleife, a circuit at the old race track at Nürburgring, Germany. Consisting of 20.83-kilometres and 73 turns, steep inclines and tricky corners, manufacturers target their fastest cars (and drivers!) to achieve the fastest lap time. The result: breath-taking speeds from many *Top Speed* cars.

Taking a corner on the Nordschleife in a Nürburgring star, the Mercedes-AMG GT R.

**A selection of Nürburgring *Top Speed* heroes 2009–2017.**

|  |  |  |
|---|---|---|
| 6 mins 43.22 secs | McLaren P1 GTR LM | 2017 |
| 6 mins 45.90 secs | NextEV NIO EP9 | 2017 |
| 6 mins 48.00 secs | Radical SR8LM | 2009 |
| 6 mins 52.01 secs | Lamborghini Huracan Performante | 2017 |
| 6 mins 57.00 secs | Porsche 918 Spyder | 2013 |
| 6 mins 59.73 secs | Lamborghini Aventador LP750-4 Superveloce | 2015 |
| 7 mins 03.45 secs | Dodge Viper SRT-10 ACR Extreme | 2017 |
| 7 mins 08.68 secs | Nissan GT-R Nismo | 2015 |
| 7 mins 10.92 secs | Mercedes-AMG GT R | 2017 |
| 7 mins 12.70 secs | Porsche 911 GT3 | 2017 |
| 7 mins 16.00 secs | Chevrolet Camaro ZL1 1LE | 2017 |
| 7 mins 21.63 secs | Ferrari 488 GTB | 2015 |
| 7 mins 27.88 secs | BMW M4 GTS | 2016 |
| 7 mins 32.00 secs | Alfa Romeo Giulia Quadrifoglio | 2016 |
| 7 mins 32.19 secs | Ford Shelby GT350R | 2015 |
| 7 mins 38.00 secs | Porsche Panamera Turbo | 2017 |
| 7 mins 43.80 secs | Honda Civic Type R | 2017 |
| 7 mins 47.19 secs | Volkswagen Golf GTI Clubsport S | 2016 |
| 7 mins 54.36 secs | Renault Mégane RS 275 Trophy-R | 2015 |
| 7 mins 59.74 secs | Porsche Cayenne Turbo S | 2016 |

Source: https://nurburgringlaptimes.com

# Pocket Rockets

> A pocket rocket is a small car that has big ambitions – high top speed, great handling and really fast acceleration. Turbocharging means even tiny engines can deliver big power, while upgraded brakes and fat tyres guarantee they stop as well as they go. At heart they might be the same as other models in their range with much less power, but a true pocket rocket will always stand out. Alloy wheels, spoilers, a spine-tingling exhaust note and even racing stripes all play their part in making these rockets roar!

# RenaultSport Clio 220 Trophy

**Country of manufacture | France**

Few companies know as much about making a pocket rocket go and handle beautifully as RenaultSport. They have come up with classics over the years, and the latest is uprated in all the right places to be a bundle of fun on twisty roads. Purists bemoan the paddle-shift auto, but there's Race mode and Launch control...

The facelifted front end of this Clio has new headlights that will light up the night with nine LEDs and six reflectors. Also note the chequered flag-inspired pattern on the bumper. Nice touch!

## Performance

| | |
|---|---|
| Top speed | 146 mph |
| 0–62 mph | 6.6 secs |
| Power | 220 hp |
| Torque | 280 Nm |

## Engine

| | |
|---|---|
| Capacity | 1.6-litre 4 cylinder |
| Type | Turbocharged |

## Efficiency

| | |
|---|---|
| Mileage | 47.9 mpg |

## Dimensions

| | |
|---|---|
| Kerb weight | 1,204 kg |
| Power/weight | 183 hp/tonne |
| Length | 4,063 mm |

# Mini John Cooper Works

| Country of manufacture | United Kingdom |
| --- | --- |

Minis aren't as mini as they used to be but they are just as sporty! The quickest is the John Cooper Works. It gets a bigger 2.0-litre engine than the 1.6 Cooper S, sports suspension and a choice of manual or auto transmission. We suggest the paddle-shift auto: it's two-tenths of a second quicker than the manual 'box!

See this badge on the front of a Mini and you'll know it's fast! 'Works' was the name of the hotted-up Mini Coopers of the 1960s.

## Performance

| | |
| --- | --- |
| Top speed | 153 mph |
| 0–62 mph | 6.1 secs |
| Power | 231 hp |
| Torque | 320 Nm |

## Engine

| | |
| --- | --- |
| Capacity | 2.0-litre 4 cylinder |
| Type | Turbocharged |

## Efficiency

| | |
| --- | --- |
| Mileage | 49.6 mpg |

## Dimensions

| | |
| --- | --- |
| Kerb weight | 1,295 kg |
| Power/weight | 178 hp/tonne |
| Length | 3,874 mm |

# Audi S1 quattro Competition

| Country of manufacture | Belgium |
| --- | --- |

It may be Audi's smallest car but there's nothing junior about the S1 quattro, especially in sporty Competition form. It is as at home in day-to-day driving as it is sprinting round a circuit, and quattro all-wheel drive means it can do it all rain or shine. With the Golf GTI engine and a six-speed manual gearbox, it's a mini-beast!

Sporty five-spoke wheels do a good job setting off S1's design – and a great job showing off the smallest Audi's red painted brake calipers!

## Performance

| | |
| --- | --- |
| Top speed | 155 mph |
| 0–62 mph | 5.8 secs |
| Power | 231 hp |
| Torque | 370 Nm |

## Engine

| | |
| --- | --- |
| Capacity | 2.0-litre 4 cylinder |
| Type | Turbocharged |

## Efficiency

| | |
| --- | --- |
| Mileage | 39.8 mpg |

## Dimensions

| | |
| --- | --- |
| Kerb weight | 1,315 kg |
| Power/weight | 176 hp/tonne |
| Length | 3,975 mm |

# Vauxhall/Opel Corsa VXR

**Countries of manufacture** | **Germany and Spain**

The hottest little Vauxhall/Opel pocket rocket used to wear Nürburgring badges, which tells you something about its performance aspirations. The badge may be no more – it's just plain Corsa VXR now – but all the good bits of the 'Ring pack are present: 205-hp turbo 1.6 motor, lowered suspension and Recaro seats.

Even though not the fastest anymore, the VXR is a driver's delight. Its cricket ball-sized gearknob and pocket rocket dials can be admired from the Recaro sports seats that will hold you rock steady during cornering.

 **Performance**

| | |
|---|---|
| Top speed | 143 mph |
| 0–62 mph | 6.8 secs |
| Power | 205 hp |
| Torque | 280 Nm |

 **Engine**

| | |
|---|---|
| Capacity | 1.6-litre 4 cylinder |
| Type | Turbocharged |

 **Efficiency**

| | |
|---|---|
| Mileage | 37.7 mpg |

 **Dimensions**

| | |
|---|---|
| Kerb weight | 1,278 kg |
| Power/weight | 160 hp/tonne |
| Length | 4,036 mm |

# Smart Fortwo Brabus

| Country of manufacture | France |
|---|---|

Brabus is famous for 900-hp Merc conversions and other specials that rank among the world's fastest conversions. The German tuning firm also waves its performance wand over this: a tiny city car with a 900-cc three-cylinder engine in the back. It's the Smart Fortwo, and while it only has 109 hp it does have Race Start mode!

It might have half the power of other pocket rockets, but the Brabus isn't short on attitude – inside and outside.

 **Performance**

| | |
|---|---|
| Top speed | 103 mph |
| 0–62 mph | 9.5 secs |
| Power | 109 hp |
| Torque | 170 Nm |

 **Engine**

| | |
|---|---|
| Capacity | 900-cc 3 cylinder |
| Type | Turbocharged |

 **Efficiency**

| | |
|---|---|
| Mileage | 62.8 mpg |

 **Dimensions**

| | |
|---|---|
| Kerb weight | 995 kg |
| Power/weight | 108 hp/tonne |
| Length | 2,740 mm |

# Volkswagen Polo GTI

**Country of manufacture** | **Spain**

The VW Polo is growing up! After 14 million cars and five generations it's certainly time. The all-new GTI with 2.0-litre TSI engine and 200 hp promises to be the sportiest Polo ever. The same size as a 2004 Golf, it has a digital dashboard, GTI-style trim and either six-speed manual or seven-speed DSG transmission.

New MkVI Polo GTI ditches the previous 1.8-litre engine for the more powerful 2.0-litre turbo.

 **Performance**

| | |
|---|---|
| Top speed | 147 mph* |
| 0–62 mph | 6.7 secs* |
| Power | 200 hp |
| Torque | 250 Nm* |

 **Engine**

| | |
|---|---|
| Capacity | 2.0-litre 4 cylinder |
| Type | Turbocharged |

 **Efficiency**

| | |
|---|---|
| Mileage | 50.4 mpg* |

 **Dimensions**

| | |
|---|---|
| Kerb weight | 1,280 kg* |
| Power/weight | 150 hp/tonne* |
| Length | 4,053 mm |

Note: * = figures for 1.8 version; new model details not available.

# Ford Fiesta ST200

**Country of manufacture** | **Global sites**

Keen drivers the world over have decided: for all-round ability the ST200 is a five-star champion. There are faster pocket rockets but probably none that handle as sweetly or come with as few compromises for every day use – quite a claim even for a car like Fiesta with so many revered hot versions over the years.

Carbon-fibre dashboard inserts, alloy-metal pedals and gearshifter, and an ST-specification steering wheel are just a few of the ST200's home comforts. But don't get too comfy – there's a new Fiesta ready to roll out of the factory!

 **Performance**

| Top speed | 143 mph |
| 0–62 mph | 6.7 secs |
| Power | 200 hp |
| Torque | 290 Nm |

 **Engine**

| Capacity | 1.6-litre 4 cylinder |
| Type | Turbocharged |

 **Efficiency**

| Mileage | 46.3 mpg |

 **Dimensions**

| Kerb weight | 1,575 kg |
| Power/weight | 127 hp/tonne |
| Length | 3,982 mm |

# Abarth 695 Biposto

| Country of manufacture | Italy |

Italians love small cars and they love motor racing – put them together and you get the 695 Biposto. It's a Fiat 500 two-seater and the closest thing you can get to a mini race car for the road. With Brembo brakes, adjustable suspension, racing gearbox and more, it's top Italian *brio* – with a great exhaust note to boot!

The 'Abarth Corsa by Sabelt' special edition with its four-point seat belts, polycarbonate windows, OZ wheels and titanium wheel bolts is so race spec that you might feel under dressed behind the wheel without an Arai helmet.

###  Performance

| | |
|---|---|
| Top speed | 143 mph |
| 0–62 mph | 5.9 secs |
| Power | 190 hp |
| Torque | 250 Nm |

### Engine

| | |
|---|---|
| Capacity | 1.4-litre 4 cylinder |
| Type | Turbocharged |

### Efficiency

| | |
|---|---|
| Mileage | 45.6 mpg |

###   Dimensions

| | |
|---|---|
| Kerb weight | 997 kg |
| Power/weight | 189 hp/tonne |
| Length | 3,657 mm |

# Hot Hatches

▶ Inside every tame family hatchback lurks a rip-roaring sports machine! Three- or five-door hot hatchbacks, or sport compacts, existed before the 1976 VW Golf GTI but this was the car that really put hot hatches on the map. And they haven't looked back since. Today they use turbochargers to extract huge horsepower from mostly four-cylinder engines, and with advanced suspensions and aerodynamics they are faster than many sports cars – but still offer room for the family!

# Nissan Juke-R 2.0

**Country of manufacture** | **United Kingdom**

It's the maddest hot hatch ever – a Nissan Juke crossed with a Nissan GT-R supercar – with almost 600 hp and awesome acceleration! It started as a concept car but some people had to have one, whatever it cost. Under the wild body it is all GT-R, including all-wheel drive – which it definitely needs with all that power!

Twin rear carbon-fibre winglets make a very purposeful addition to the Juke R's style – as well as creating some downforce at speed. And speed is what this thing's all about! This car is so specialized, many details are kept under wraps.

## Performance

| | |
|---|---|
| Top speed | 160 mph plus |
| 0–60 mph | 3.3 secs |
| Power | 592 hp |
| Torque | 652 Nm |

## Engine

| | |
|---|---|
| Capacity | 3.8-litre V6 |
| Type | Twin turbocharged |

## Efficiency

| | |
|---|---|
| Mileage | Not available |

## Dimensions

| | |
|---|---|
| Kerb weight | Not available |
| Power/weight | Not available |
| Length | Not available |

# Ford Focus RS

| Country of manufacture | Germany |

RS is Ford's recipe for driving bliss. But with more power than ever something had to be done to keep the wild child from misbehaving. So the handling has been tamed with all-wheel drive, making it much more usable on all roads. There's even a Drift button – here's a 4x4 hot hatch that can oversteer like a muscle car.

Body-hugging Recaro seats and a manual gearbox are icing on the Focus RS cake. And did you know that Ford's 'engine listeners' check each 2.3-litre unit to make sure the 320-hp engine is in the peak of good health?

 **Performance**

| | |
|---|---|
| Top speed | 165 mph |
| 0–62 mph | 4.7 secs |
| Power | 320 hp |
| Torque | 470 Nm |

 **Engine**

| | |
|---|---|
| Capacity | 2.3-litre 4 cylinder |
| Type | Turbocharged |

 **Efficiency**

| | |
|---|---|
| Mileage | 36.7 mpg |

 **Dimensions**

| | |
|---|---|
| Kerb weight | 1,547 kg |
| Power/weight | 207 hp/tonne |
| Length | 4,390 mm |

# RenaultSport Mégane 275 Trophy-R

**Country of manufacture** | **France**

The first front-driver to break eight minutes at the Nürburgring in 2014, the Trophy-R is the ultimate Mégane. The R (two seats and full roll cage) is a limited edition but the regular Trophy has the same 275 horses. In 2017 an all-new version brings four-wheel steering and a choice of manual or paddle-shift dual-clutch gearbox.

Alloy pedals and white-faced dials do their best to sportify the Mégane's now-dated interior. The new version will improve things, and gets paddle-shift auto as well as manual gearbox. It will be out to get its 'Ring record back!

 **Performance**

| | |
|---|---|
| Top speed | 158 mph |
| 0–62 mph | 5.8 secs |
| Power | 275 hp |
| Torque | 360 Nm |

 **Engine**

| | |
|---|---|
| Capacity | 2.0-litre 4 cylinder |
| Type | Turbocharged |

 **Efficiency**

| | |
|---|---|
| Mileage | 37.7 mpg |

 **Dimensions**

| | |
|---|---|
| Kerb weight | 1,297 kg |
| Power/weight | 212 hp/tonne |
| Length | 4,330 mm |

# Seat Leon SC CUPRA R

**ountry of manufacture | Spain**

CUPRA has long been Spanish for sporty Seats, and the spicier the better. The Leon SC is the hottest of them all – with 300 hp it's the most powerful Seat ever. It comes in both front-drive and (in the ST estate version) all-wheel drive forms, and also with a choice of body styles and either manual or paddle-shift auto 'boxes.

Chequered flag badge is not just for show: this Spanish flyer was honed at the Nürburgring. Seat offers lots of model choice – all with a tasty 300 hp!

###  Performance

| | |
|---|---|
| Top speed | 155 mph |
| 0–62 mph | 5.6 secs |
| Power | 300 hp |
| Torque | 380 Nm |

### Engine

| | |
|---|---|
| Capacity | 2.0- litre 4 cylinder |
| Type | Turbocharged |

###  Efficiency

| | |
|---|---|
| Mileage | 42.2 mpg |

###  Dimensions

| | |
|---|---|
| Kerb weight | 1,395 kg |
| Power/weight | 215 hp/tonne |
| Length | 4,246 mm |

# Honda Civic Type R

**Country of manufacture** | **United Kingdom**

'Type R' is part of hot hatch legend. The sporty Civic in its most powerful form re-invented the breed in the 1990s, captivating fans who were distraught when Honda stopped making it. Now the winged wonder is back and the latest 2018 version is setting the pace. Turbocharged and front-wheel drive, it'll do almost 170 mph!

It's a mix of vents, scoops, strakes, wings, bumps and edges and even a triple bazooka exhaust. Vortex generators at the roof's back edge channel airflow toward the Type R's huge rear wing.

## Performance

| | |
|---|---|
| Top speed | 169 mph |
| 0–62 mph | 5.8 secs |
| Power | 320 hp |
| Torque | 400 Nm |

## Engine

| | |
|---|---|
| Capacity | 2.0-litre 4 cylinder |
| Type | Turbocharged |

## Efficiency

| | |
|---|---|
| Mileage | 36.7 mpg |

## Dimensions

| | |
|---|---|
| Kerb weight | 1,380 kg |
| Power/weight | 232 hp/tonne |
| Length | 4,557 mm |

# Peugeot 308 GTi

| Country of manufacture | France |
| --- | --- |

If VW's Golf was the first hot hatch, then Peugeot's influential 205 GTi of the 1980s is usually said to be the best. Fast and agile, it could be a handful in the corners but get it right and the rewards were immense. Also fast and agile, but no way a handful, is today's hot Pug. The 308 GTi is a talented all-rounder.

GTi by name, GTi by nature: latest hot 308 marks return to form for the French firm – even if one of the options for the car is the odd 'Coupe Franche' two-colour paint job.

## Performance

| | |
| --- | --- |
| Top speed | 155 mph |
| 0–60 mph | 6.0 secs |
| Power | 272 hp |
| Torque | 330 Nm |

## Engine

| | |
| --- | --- |
| Capacity | 1.6-litre 4 cylinder |
| Type | Turbocharged |

## Efficiency

| | |
| --- | --- |
| Mileage | 47.1 mpg |

## Dimensions

| | |
| --- | --- |
| Kerb weight | 1,205 kg |
| Power/weight | 226 hp/tonne |
| Length | 4,253 mm |

# BMW M140i

BMW's baby M car is the M2, a sedan. If you want a hatch, and a hot one, it has to be this. The M140i has a big engine for a small car and goes for creamy delivery more than outright power, but even so is delightfully fast and refined with handing to-die-for. Plus it makes one of the best noises in all of motoring!

BMW's M140i is a bit of a Q car to look at, but it can really light up your drive with its smooth six-cylinder power and rear-wheel drive handling. It's all proper old-school!

 **Performance**

| | |
|---|---|
| Top speed | 155 mph |
| 0–62 mph | 4.8 secs |
| Power | 340 hp |
| Torque | 500 Nm |

 **Engine**

| | |
|---|---|
| Capacity | 3.0-litre 6 cylinder |
| Type | Turbocharged |

 **Efficiency**

| | |
|---|---|
| Mileage | 36.2 mpg |

 **Dimensions**

| | |
|---|---|
| Kerb weight | 1,520 kg |
| Power/weight | 224 hp/tonne |
| Length | 4,324 mm |

# Mercedes-AMG A45

| Country of manufacture | Germany |
|---|---|

Mercedes isn't the first name to come to mind where hot hatches are concerned. But the AMG A45 is certainly a hatchback, and with a mind-boggling 381 hp from just 2.0-litres it is definitely hot! With all-wheel drive and lots of electronic stability systems, it can get its power down with precision yet still be fun to drive.

Always fast and fun, things get even more exciting (and louder!) when you push the Sport button. There's also a Sport Handling mode for when you want to hang the tail out.

###  Performance

| | |
|---|---|
| Top speed | 155 mph |
| 0–62 mph | 4.2 secs |
| Power | 381 hp |
| Torque | 475 Nm |

###  Engine

| | |
|---|---|
| Capacity | 2.0-litre 4 cylinder |
| Type | Turbocharged |

### Efficiency

| | |
|---|---|
| Mileage | 40.9 mpg |

###  Dimensions

| | |
|---|---|
| Kerb weight | 1,555 kg |
| Power/weight | 245 hp/tonne |
| Length | 4,299 mm |

# VW Golf GTI Clubsport S

**Country of manufacture** | **Germany**

The daddy of all hot hatches is scorching when in Clubsport S form. The most powerful GTI ever smashed the Nürburgring lap record for front-drive cars in 2016 and even comes with a special handling setting tailored to the 'Ring. The three-door, two-seater ultimate GTI is as much of a hit on public roads.

There are only seats upfront in this GTI. Part of VW's weight-loss strategy was to lose the two back seats, but this Nürburgring driver doesn't seem to mind.

## Performance

| | |
|---|---|
| Top speed | 165 mph |
| 0–62 mph | 5.9 secs |
| Power | 310 hp |
| Torque | 380 Nm |

## Engine

| | |
|---|---|
| Capacity | 2.0-litre 4 cylinder |
| Type | Turbocharged |

## Efficiency

| | |
|---|---|
| Mileage | 38.2 mpg |

## Dimensions

| | |
|---|---|
| Kerb weight | 1,360 kg |
| Power/weight | 228 hp/tonne |
| Length | 4,268 mm |

# Audi RS3 quattro

**Country of manufacture | Germany**

Turbocharged, four-wheel drive and with an inline five-cylinder engine – it could be the original Audi Quattro. While the new version still boasts the five-pot exhaust beat, it comes with twice the power! With the charismatic quick-shifting S-Tronic dual-clutch automatic transmission, its 400 hp makes it super-fast.

The S-Tronic seven-speed dual-clutch transmission and permanent all-wheel drive transfer the power of the five cylinders to the wheels. The sportier the driving, the more torque hits the rear axle.

 **Performance**

| | |
|---|---|
| Top speed | 155 mph |
| 0–62 mph | 4.1 secs |
| Power | 400 hp |
| Torque | 480 Nm |

 **Engine**

| | |
|---|---|
| Capacity | 2.5-litre 5 cylinder |
| Type | Turbocharged |

 **Efficiency**

| | |
|---|---|
| Mileage | 34.0 mpg |

 **Dimensions**

| | |
|---|---|
| Kerb weight | 1,510 kg |
| Power/weight | 265 hp/tonne |
| Length | 4,335 mm |

# Speedy SUVs

 Welcome to the world of the performance giants! Sport utility vehicles grew out of what is called in the USA the light truck segment, but there's nothing truck-like about these monsters. From humble 4x4 beginnings SUVs, or crossovers, have grown into the largest, most powerful, luxurious and expensive cars on the planet with all-terrain capability and a feel-good factor that only sitting up high above everyone else can give. All the big names are in – there's even a Rolls-Royce SUV on its way!

# Audi SQ7

| Country of manufacture | Slovakia |

Seven-seat diesel 4x4s aren't what they used to be…look at Audi's flagship Q7. The three-row family wagon's twin turbo V8 diesel is boosted by an electric compressor to churn out big power and even more impressive torque. Sub 5.0 sec 0–62 mph acceleration is the order of the day, but this car can do almost 40 mpg!

The SQ7's badge holds the clue to its massive performance: V8T stands for a twin turbo V8, but there's no petrol here. This engine's a diesel!

 **Performance**

| | |
|---|---|
| Top speed | 155 mph |
| 0–62 mph | 4.9 secs |
| Power | 435 hp |
| Torque | 900 Nm |

 **Engine**

| | |
|---|---|
| Capacity | 4.0-litre V8 |
| Type | Twin turbocharged |

 **Efficiency**

| | |
|---|---|
| Mileage | 39.2 mpg |

 **Dimensions**

| | |
|---|---|
| Kerb weight | 2,330 kg |
| Power/weight | 187 hp/tonne |
| Length | 5,069 mm |

# Jaguar F-Pace S

**Country of manufacture** | **United Kingdom**

Combining all Jaguar's traditional strengths in one superlative design, the F-Pace has become the marque's biggest selling model. With 'just' 380 hp from the supercharged V6 in the S version it's not as powerful as some, but then the 0–62 mph time of 5.5 secs does come with a fuel economy of a possible 32 mpg.

The F-Pace S is a compact five-seater with plenty of appeal as well as a large dose of sports car DNA to keep the driver happy. And to remind you of its power are 20-inch five-spoke alloy wheels, red brake calipers and S badging.

 **Performance**

| Top speed | 155 mph |
|---|---|
| 0–62 mph | 5.5 secs |
| Power | 380 hp |
| Torque | 450 Nm |

 **Engine**

| Capacity | 3.0-litre V6 |
|---|---|
| Type | Supercharged |

 **Efficiency**

| Mileage | 31.7 mpg |
|---|---|

 **Dimensions**

| Kerb weight | 1,861 kg |
|---|---|
| Power/weight | 204 hp/tonne |
| Length | 4,731 mm |

# Maserati Levante S

The 'Maserati of SUVs' conjures up an image of exotic styling and sports car handling and the Levante hardly disappoints. In size and power the current range-topping S model doesn't go to the lengths of some rivals, but with a charismatic 430 hp from the twin turbo V6 it goes well, sounds great and has Italian heart.

Based on the 2011 Kubang concept car, the Levante is an SUV with real Italian heart in its beautiful design and finish. Maserati's famous Trident emblem is embossed into all the head restraints.

 **Performance**

| | |
|---|---|
| Top speed | 164 mph |
| 0–62 mph | 5.2 secs |
| Power | 430 hp |
| Torque | 600 Nm |

**Engine**

| | |
|---|---|
| Capacity | 3.0-litre V6 |
| Type | Twin turbocharged |

 **Efficiency**

| | |
|---|---|
| Mileage | 26 mpg |

 **Dimensions**

| | |
|---|---|
| Kerb weight | 2,109 kg |
| Power/weight | hp/tonne |
| Length | 5,003 mm |

# Mercedes-Maybach G650 Landaulet

**Country of manufacture** | **Germany**

This is one of the most unlikely SUV superstars. There have been luxurious and powerful versions of Merc's original 4x4 before, but nothing quite like this AMG version with open landaulet body. This extravagance boasts a biturbo V12 with 630 hp – and enough hard-core off-roading hardware to go anywhere!

Stretched wheelbase means lots of room in the back – even with the electrically adjustable seats from the S-Class fitted, and complete with massage function of course! Only 99 of these Mercs are being built.

 **Performance**

| | |
|---|---|
| Top speed | 112 mph |
| 0–62 mph | 5.8 secs |
| Power | 630 hp |
| Torque | 1,000 Nm |

 **Engine**

| | |
|---|---|
| Capacity | 6.0-litre V12 |
| Type | Twin turbocharged |

 **Efficiency**

| | |
|---|---|
| Mileage | Not available |

 **Dimensions**

| | |
|---|---|
| Kerb weight | 3,000 kg (estimate) |
| Power/weight | 191 hp/tonne (estimate) |
| Length | 5,345 mm |

# Bentley Bentayga

| Country of manufacture | United Kingdom |
| --- | --- |

It's the poshest name in SUVs by far! The Bentayga takes everything the brand is known for – including the mega 6.0-litre W12 engine – and puts it into a high-riding cocoon of the finest materials and hand-crafted luxury. Performance is simply massive, while it will also handle off-road routes with ease.

The Bentayga is like entering a parallel universe of power and refinement – but be warned, taking your seat behind the steering wheel with its famous winged B badge doesn't come cheap. This is one of the world's most expensive cars.

## Performance

| | |
| --- | --- |
| Top speed | 187 mph |
| 0–62 mph | 4.0 secs |
| Power | 608 hp |
| Torque | 900 Nm |

## Engine

| | |
| --- | --- |
| Capacity | 6.0-litre W12 |
| Type | Twin turbocharged |

## Efficiency

| | |
| --- | --- |
| Mileage | 21.6 mpg |

## Dimensions

| | |
| --- | --- |
| Kerb weight | 2,440 kg |
| Power/weight | 249 hp/tonne |
| Length | 5,141 mm |

# BMW X6 M

Country of manufacture | United States

Coupe-type styling and performance combine in BMW's flagship SUV. It looks like a power hero and goes like one. An absolute flyer in a straight line, it also goes round corners thanks to its Motorsport-honed handling. Backseat passengers might not like it, but this is an SUV you can throw around like a sports car!

Dial M for Motorsport: the gear selector proudly displays the famous M logo that has distinguished so many 'ultimate driving machines' in the past.

 **Performance**

| | |
|---|---|
| Top speed | 155 mph |
| 0–62 mph | 4.2 secs |
| Power | 575 hp |
| Torque | 750 Nm |

 **Engine**

| | |
|---|---|
| Capacity | 4.4-litre V8 |
| Type | Twin turbocharged |

 **Efficiency**

| | |
|---|---|
| Mileage | 25.4 mpg |

 **Dimensions**

| | |
|---|---|
| Kerb weight | 2,265 kg |
| Power/weight | 254 hp/tonne |
| Length | 4,909 mm |

# Tesla Model X Performance

| Country of manufacture | United States |
| --- | --- |

Tesla is surging on a wave of electric power. The Model X is billed as 'the safest, fastest and most capable sport utility vehicle in history'. It might not be as good off road as Land Rover or Jeep, but it's fast in P100D form. The Ludicrous mode unleashes all the performance with the violence of an extreme fairground ride!

Adding to Model X's brilliant craziness are its signature gullwing (falcon wing) rear doors. Mind you, they make it easy to access the third row of seats. Only 30-cm of clear space are needed each side for the doors to move up and out of the way.

 **Performance**

| | |
| --- | --- |
| Top speed | 155 mph |
| 0–62 mph | 3.1 secs |
| Power | 603 hp |
| Torque | 967 Nm |

 **Engine**

| | |
| --- | --- |
| Capacity | 100 kWh |
| Type | Dual electric motor |

 **Efficiency**

| | |
| --- | --- |
| Mileage | Not available |

 **Dimensions**

| | |
| --- | --- |
| Kerb weight | 2,439 kg |
| Power/weight | 247 hp/tonne |
| Length | 5,052 mm |

# Jeep Grand Cherokee Trackhawk

**Country of manufacture** | **United States**

In a world of fast SUVs, the 2018 Trackhawk is very FAST – as fast in fact as a Lamborghini or Ferrari supercar. For a 2.4-tonne family wagon that can go off-road, its speed is astonishing. Its secret is under the bonnet: a supercharged 6.2-litre V8, called Hellcat, delivering 707 hp and making it the most powerful SUV ever!

Hellcat is the name of the most powerful SUV's engine. Unleash all its 700-plus horsepower and this ultimate Grand Cherokee feels like it is about to take off!

### Performance

| | |
|---|---|
| Top speed | 180 mph |
| 0–60 mph | 3.5 secs |
| Power | 707 hp |
| Torque | 875 Nm |

### Engine

| | |
|---|---|
| Capacity | 6.2-litre V8 |
| Type | Supercharged |

### Efficiency

| | |
|---|---|
| Mileage | Not available |

### Dimensions

| | |
|---|---|
| Kerb weight | 2,433 kg |
| Power/weight | 290 hp/tonne |
| Length | 4,800 mm |

# Porsche Cayenne Turbo S

| Country of manufacture | Slovakia |

Few cars combine all the SUV ingredients as convincingly as the Cayenne in Turbo S form. Practical, spacious and superbly built, its turbo petrol V8 delivers performance and response to shame many a sports car. No surprise really – it's built by the same company that makes 911s, 918 Spyders and 919 Hybrid Le Mans winners!

With this monster of a turbocharged V8 under its bonnet, the Cayenne is faster than some Porsche sports cars. The big SUV also outsells the sports cars!

 **Performance**

| | |
|---|---|
| Top speed | 176 mph |
| 0–62 mph | 4.1 secs |
| Power | 570 hp |
| Torque | 800 Nm |

 **Engine**

| | |
|---|---|
| Capacity | 4.8-litre V8 |
| Type | Twin turbocharged |

 **Efficiency**

| | |
|---|---|
| Mileage | 24.6 mpg |

 **Dimensions**

| | |
|---|---|
| Kerb weight | 2,310 kg |
| Power/weight | 247 hp/tonne |
| Length | 4,855 mm |

# Land Rover Range Rover Sport SVR

**Country of manufacture** | **United Kingdom**

Despite more rivals than ever, there remains only one true global icon of the luxury SUV and that's the Range Rover. It is instantly recognizable and outstandingly capable, even when in the extreme 550 hp high-performance form of the storming SVR Range Rover Sport. Basically it is just mega!

Since Range Rover's perfect shape first appeared in 1970 – it even went into the New York Museum of Modern Art! – it has evolved through successive generations into one of the best-loved cars on the road.

 **Performance**

| | |
|---|---|
| Top speed | 162 mph |
| 0–62 mph | 4.7 secs |
| Power | 550 hp |
| Torque | 680 Nm |

 **Engine**

| | |
|---|---|
| Capacity | 5-litre V8 |
| Type | Supercharged |

 **Efficiency**

| | |
|---|---|
| Mileage | 22.1 mpg |

 **Dimensions**

| | |
|---|---|
| Kerb weight | 2,333 kg |
| Power/weight | 236 hp/tonne |
| Length | 4,872 mm |

# Road and Track Heroes

No road-registerable car is more focused on track ability than these. They are not necessarily the most powerful cars but they are among the lightest – and that gives them what every race car needs: the best possible power/weight ratio. Incredibly stiff structures and advanced suspension systems confer mechanical grip while sophisticated aerodynamics ensures they are sucked down onto the tarmac – with the result they go round corners like nothing else in this book. And yes, you can still drive them to the shops!

# Caterham Seven 620R

**Country of manufacture** | **United Kingdom**

Caterham is the original supercar-slayer! For decades now its take on the original Lotus 7 has thrilled on road and track, the thrill likened to that of a high performance motorbike. The 620R is the ultimate Caterham, and the first with a supercharged engine. Combined with light weight, it offers astonishing performance.

The 620R's carbon seats each feature four-point racing harnesses to hold you securely in place on a circuit. And it's only on a circuit that the 620R's massive performance can safely be used

 **Performance**

| | |
|---|---|
| Top speed | 155 mph |
| 0–60 mph | 2.79 secs |
| Power | 310 hp |
| Torque | 297 Nm |

**Engine**

| | |
|---|---|
| Capacity | 2.0-litre 4 cylinder |
| Type | Supercharged |

 **Efficiency**

| | |
|---|---|
| Mileage | Not available |

**Dimensions**

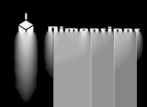

# BAC Mono

| Country of manufacture | United Kingdom |

Created with the aim of making the purest driving experience going, the Mono doesn't even have a passenger seat! It is crafted out of carbon fibre with a 2.5-litre engine and racing-style sequential gearbox. With its huge power-to-weight ratio and balance, it's a road car that can take apart a circuit like a real racer.

Exposed on either side of the bonnet are the race-spec pushrods of the Mono's twin-wishbone suspension. These give it F1-style grip even though it doesn't have an F1-style front wing, which is illegal on any road car.

 **Performance**

| | |
|---|---|
| Top speed | 170 mph |
| 0–62 mph | 2.8 secs |
| Power | 309 hp |
| Torque | 308 Nm |

 **Engine**

| | |
|---|---|
| Capacity | 2.5-litre 4 cylinder |
| Type | Naturally aspirated |

 **Efficiency**

| | |
|---|---|
| Mileage | 42.2 mpg |

 **Dimensions**

| | |
|---|---|
| Kerb weight | 580 kg |
| Power/weight | 533 hp/tonne |
| Length | 3,952 mm |

# Radical RXC Turbo 600R

| Country of manufacture | United Kingdom |
|---|---|

In just 20 years the Radical has become the road and track machine to beat. Light, powerful and with high downforce, the cars are virtually Le Mans racers for the road! In 2009 an SR8 was driven from the UK to the Nürburgring where it set a record that stood for years. The 600R corners at 2g, putting the SR8 in the shade!

Inside the cockpit, accessed via the gullwing doors, there are Alcantara Radical embroidered Corbeau seats and Alcantara finish. On the dash of this special edition is a 20th anniversary plaque marking the 2,000th Radical manufactured.

## Performance

| | |
|---|---|
| Top speed | 180 mph |
| 0–60 mph | 2.7 secs |
| Power | 537 hp |
| Torque | 650 Nm |

## Engine

| | |
|---|---|
| Capacity | 3.5-litre V6 |
| Type | Twin turbocharged |

## Efficiency

| | |
|---|---|
| Mileage | Not available |

## Dimensions

| | |
|---|---|
| Kerb weight | 1,130 kg |
| Power/weight | 575 hp/tonne |
| Length | 4,300 mm |

# Ariel Atom 3.5

**Country of manufacture** | **United Kingdom**

No, they didn't forget to put the bodywork on, the Atom comes like this! The motorcycle-inspired skeletal frame is all about strength (and safety) without weight, and so what if you get wet if it rains. The Atom's figures show how successful the formula is. Ariel's 'serious fun' extends to an off-road version called Nomad.

Flip the ignition switch, and the LCD dash springs to life, the shift lights flash and the fuel pump primes. Press the starter, and the engine instantly fires – ready for track action or city traffic.

 **Performance**

| | |
|---|---|
| Top speed | 145 mph |
| 0–62 mph | 3.1 secs |
| Power | 245 hp |
| Torque | 210 Nm |

 **Engine**

| | |
|---|---|
| Capacity | 2.0-litre 4 cylinder |
| Type | Naturally aspirated |

**Efficiency**

| | |
|---|---|
| Mileage | 31.4 mpg |

 **Dimensions**

| | |
|---|---|
| Kerb weight | 620 kg |
| Power/weight | 471 hp/tonne |
| Length | 3,410 mm |

# KTM X-Bow R

For almost 10 years the X-Bow (crossbow) has delighted drivers with its 21st century take on the simple but effective sports car, as championed by Lotus since the 1950s. Inspired by advanced aerodynamics and carbon-fibre construction from the world of motor racing, it is a usable sports car and track-day weapon.

When launched in 2008 it was the world's first production car with full carbon composite monocoque. While the underbody is completely flat F1-style, the rear end is a layer cake of foils, flaps and exposed carbon-fibre tub.

## Performance

| | |
|---|---|
| Top speed | 143 mph |
| 0–62 mph | 3.9 secs |
| Power | 300 hp |
| Torque | 400 Nm |

## Engine

| | |
|---|---|
| Capacity | 2.0-litre 4 cylinder |
| Type | Turbocharged |

## Efficiency

| | |
|---|---|
| Mileage | 34 mpg |

## Dimensions

| | |
|---|---|
| Kerb weight | 790 kg |
| Power/weight | 380 hp/tonne |
| Length | 3,738 mm |

# otus 3-Eleven

Lotus has a reputation for fast road cars and fast racing cars. In the amazing 3-Eleven it has a car that is fast and massively capable on road and track. This is the most driver focused Lotus ever. It follows in the tyretracks of the highly sought-after Lotus 2-Eleven, but updates the formula with more power and fresh design.

The 3-Eleven – with a planned production run of just 311 cars – has gloss black forged wheels and red AP Racing four-piston calipers. The front splitter, along with rear wing and diffuser, produces 150 kg of downforce at 150 mph.

 **Performance**

| | |
|---|---|
| Top speed | 174 mph |
| 0–62 mph | 3.4 secs |
| Power | 410 hp |
| Torque | 410 Nm |

 **Engine**

| | |
|---|---|
| Capacity | 3.5-litre V6 |
| Type | Supercharged |

 **Efficiency**

| | |
|---|---|
| Mileage | Not available |

 **Dimensions**

| | |
|---|---|
| Kerb weight | 925 kg |
| Power/weight | 443 hp/tonne |
| Length | 4,080 mm |

# Caparo T1

Country of manufacture | United Kingdom

Street-legal racing cars come no racier. The T1's power-to-weight ratio is off the scale, due to its light weight and V8 with 583 hp. The result? Mind-bending performance; 5-sec 0–100 mph is claimed. The T1's evolution has been rocky but it is an astonishing machine from some of the people behind the McLaren F1.

The heart of the T1's powertrain is the all-aluminium 90-degree V8. On standard fuel it claims 583 hp, but put methanol in it and it puts out 700 hp!

 **Performance**

| | |
|---|---|
| Top speed | 205 mph |
| 0–62 mph | 2.5 secs |
| Power | 583 hp |
| Torque | 420 Nm |

**Engine**

| | |
|---|---|
| Capacity | 3.5-litre V8 |
| Type | Naturally aspirated |

 **Efficiency**

| | |
|---|---|
| Mileage | Not available |

 **Dimensions**

| | |
|---|---|
| Kerb weight | 470 kg |
| Power/weight | 1,240 hp/tonne |
| Length | 4,066 mm |

# Elemental RP1

| Country of manufacture | United Kingdom |

Extreme aerodynamics and light weight are the key to the RP1, the newest road and track car. The doorless two-seater, with a legs-up driving position like that of a Formula 1 car, is the work of mostly ex-McLaren engineers well versed in making cars go fast. Its targets, like 0–100 mph in 6.4 secs, will surely make it front of the grid.

The hybrid carbon fibre/aluminium composite tub structure of the RP1, the radical underfloor downforce-generating aerodynamics and lightweight chassis make the RP1 a game-changer in car design.

 **Performance**

| | |
|---|---|
| Top speed | 165 mph |
| 0–62 mph | 2.8 secs |
| Power | 320 hp |
| Torque | 435 Nm |

 **Engine**

| | |
|---|---|
| Capacity | 2.0-litre 4 cylinder |
| Type | Turbocharged |

 **Efficiency**

| | |
|---|---|
| Mileage | Not available |

 **Dimensions**

| | |
|---|---|
| Kerb weight | 580 kg |
| Power/weight | 551 hp/tonne |
| Length | 3,740 mm |

# Fast GTs

*Gran turismo...* just the name conjures up speed, luxury and sophistication, all the attributes necessary for blasting across continents to exotic locations. GTs can be just as fast and sporty as out-and-out supercars, but with 2+2 cabins and luggage space are far more accommodating. And they can be just as luxurious as limousines, but with their two-door bodies look a whole lot more seductive! No wonder some GTs have become the most iconic cars in all of high performance motoring.

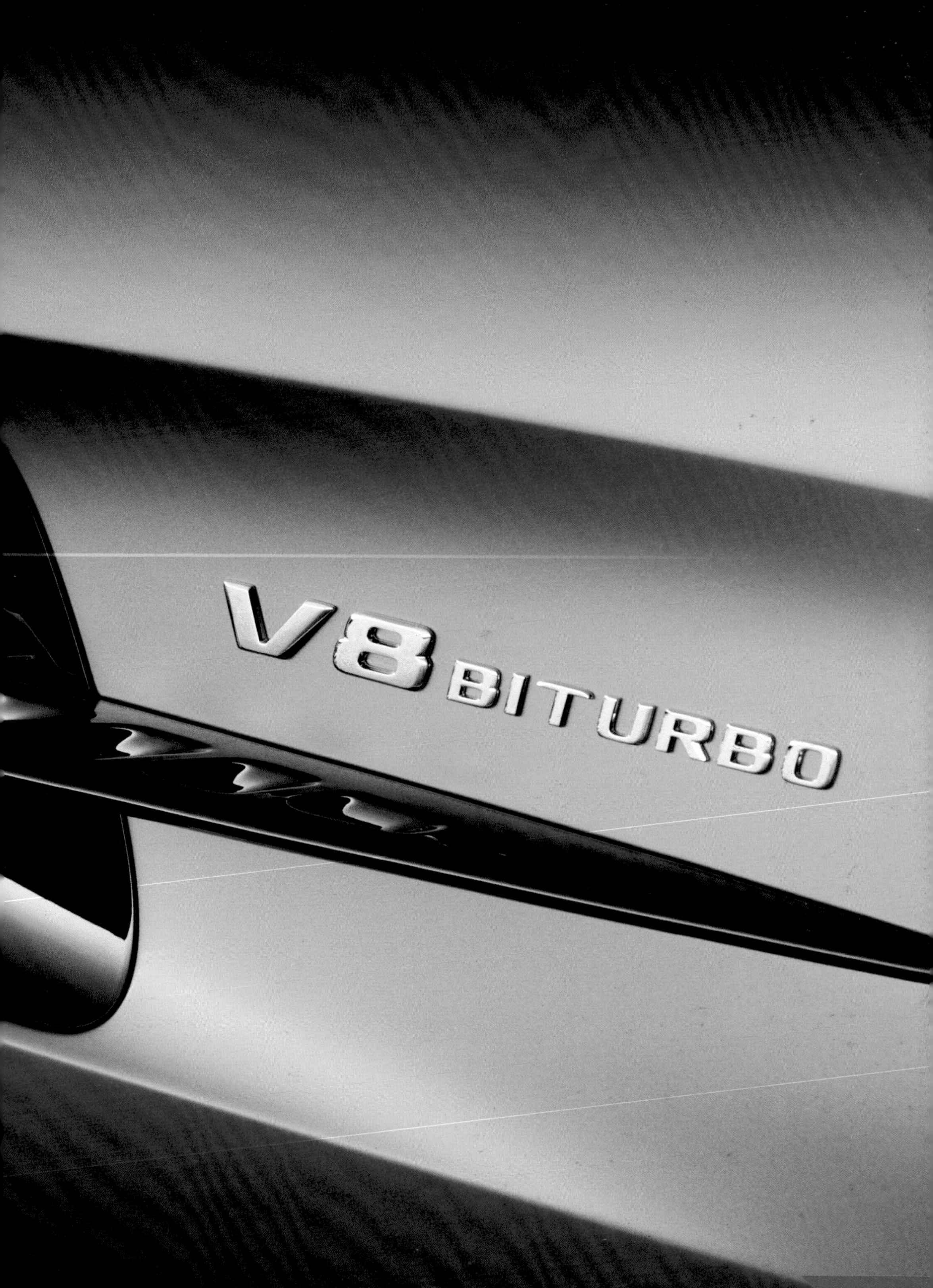
V8 BITURBO

# Ferrari 812 Superfast

**Country of manufacture** | **Italy**

The classic front-engine, rear-drive Ferrari *gran turismo* is alive and well, and faster than ever. The 812 Superfast is the most powerful and fastest Ferrari in full production. There are no turbos or electric motors, just traditional V12 grunt and 8,500 rpm limit! A 'successor' to the Daytona, the Superfast lives up to its name!

The spacious interior, comfortable driving position and excellent visibility to the front and sides all add to the 812's approachability. And how how reassuring is that black prancing horse?

## Performance

| | |
|---|---|
| Top speed | 211 mph |
| 0–62 mph | 2.9 secs |
| Power | 800 hp |
| Torque | 719 Nm |

## Engine

| | |
|---|---|
| Capacity | 6.5-litre V12 |
| Type | Naturally aspirated |

## Efficiency

| | |
|---|---|
| Mileage | 19 mpg |

## Dimensions

| | |
|---|---|
| Kerb weight | 1,525 kg |
| Power/weight | 525 hp/tonne |
| Length | 4,656 mm |

# Rolls-Royce Wraith

| Country of manufacture | United Kingdom |
| --- | --- |

Famed for its silence and luxury, the Rolls-Royce is more of a driver's car than ever these days. The V12 engine has always been amply endowed, but now a semi-sporting chassis harnesses the power to surprising effect in the two-door Wraith. In Black Badge form, a dark, moody character meets majestic performance.

The Black Badge Wraith may have been designed for risk takers who laugh in the face of convention, but it's usually revered respect that is aroused when the Spirit of Ectasy goddess wafts by. With 0–62 mph in 4.5 secs 'speeds by' would be more accurate.

 **Performance**

| Top speed | 155 mph |
| --- | --- |
| 0–62 mph | 4.5 secs |
| Power | 632 hp |
| Torque | 870 Nm |

 **Engine**

| Capacity | 6.6-litre V12 |
| --- | --- |
| Type | Twin turbocharged |

 **Efficiency**

| Mileage | 19.3 mpg |
| --- | --- |

 **Dimensions**

| Kerb weight | 2,440 kg |
| --- | --- |
| Power/weight | 259 hp/tonne |
| Length | 5,285 mm |

# Lexus LC500h

**Country of manufacture** | **Japan**

This is the car Lexus believes is going to make Porsche drivers think twice! The LC500h is sure to be noticed, with its distinctively different looks and mechanical package. The 'h' stands for hybrid, a combination of turbo V6 and electric motor. It's even got two transmissions: a CVT and a regular automatic.

The 500h is a tangle of sharp edges and intersecting lines, but take details like the grille, shallow headlights, front wings that hug the wheels, floating roof and 3D-effect rear lights and there's much to admire.

## Performance

| | |
|---|---|
| Top speed | 155 mph |
| 0–60 mph | 4.7 secs |
| Power | 359 hp |
| Torque | 380 Nm (petrol), 300 Nm (electric) |

## Engine

| | |
|---|---|
| Capacity | 3.5-litre V6 |
| Type | Petrol/electric hybrid |

## Efficiency

| | |
|---|---|
| Mileage | 39 mpg |

## Dimensions

| | |
|---|---|
| Kerb weight | 2,012 kg |
| Power/weight | 176 hp/tonne |
| Length | 4,760 mm |

# Aston Martin DB11

| Country of manufacture | United Kingdom |

Aston Martin's new era of cars starts with the DB11. It builds on the power, beauty and raw charisma of its forebears with a new twin-turbo V12 power, clever aerodynamics and stunning looks. The revolution in its electronics is due to parts-sharing with Mercedes. You can even get a DB11 with an AMG V8!

Rear-end lift is reduced by the DB11's AeroBlade, a concealed 'virtual' spoiler that is fed by air intakes at the base of each C-pillar. Air is ducted through the bodywork, before venting as a jet of air from the aperture in the rear decklid.

## Performance

| | |
|---|---|
| Top speed | 200 mph |
| 0–62 mph | 3.9 secs |
| Power | 608 hp |
| Torque | 700 Nm |

## Engine

| | |
|---|---|
| Capacity | 5.2-litre V12 |
| Type | Twin turbocharged |

## Efficiency

| | |
|---|---|
| Mileage | 24.8 mpg |

## Dimensions

| | |
|---|---|
| Kerb weight | 1,770 kg |
| Power/weight | 344 hp/tonne |
| Length | 4,739 mm |

# Nissan GT-R Nismo

| Country of manufacture | Japan |
| --- | --- |

It's 'Godzilla' in its most extreme form yet! Japan's distinctively angular 2+2 all-wheel drive coupe has been thrilling drivers on road and track for 10 years now, and it just gets better. Fettled by Nissan tuning arm Nismo, the best GT-R today boasts 600 hp and acceleration right up there with the world's fastest supercars.

Each Nissan GT-R engine is hand-assembled by a single technician (a dash plaque bears his or her signature) in a dust- and temperature-controlled clean room much like those used for Formula One racing engines. And this in a car you can drive to work in every day!

## Performance

| | |
| --- | --- |
| Top speed | 196 mph |
| 0–60 mph | 2.5 secs |
| Power | 600 hp |
| Torque | 652 Nm |

## Engine

| | |
| --- | --- |
| Capacity | 3.8-litre V6 |
| Type | Twin-turbocharged |

## Efficiency

| | |
| --- | --- |
| Mileage | 23.9 mpg |

## Dimensions

| | |
| --- | --- |
| Kerb weight | 1,725 kg |
| Power/weight | 348 hp/tonne |
| Length | 4,690 mm |

# Bentley Continental GT Supersports

**Country of manufacture** | **United Kingdom**

Bentley's resurgence as part of the VW empire is down to the Continental GT, and with models like the Supersports its appeal just increases. The W12 engine is in its most powerful-ever form here, and with a torque vectoring system from the GT3 race car, the all-wheel drive Supersports handles the 710 hp with aplomb.

The Supersports has high-performance carbon ceramic brakes – the discs are the largest of their type in the world – and a cool carbon-fibre rear spoiler, but do you care when wrapped in diamond-quilted leather and Alcantara luxury?

 **Performance**

| | |
|---|---|
| Top speed | 209 mph |
| 0–62 mph | 3.5 secs |
| Power | 710 hp |
| Torque | 1,017 Nm |

**Engine**

| | |
|---|---|
| Capacity | 6.0-litre 12 cylinder |
| Type | Twin turbocharged |

 **Efficiency**

| | |
|---|---|
| Mileage | 18.0 mpg |

**Dimensions**

| | |
|---|---|
| Kerb weight | 2,280 kg |
| Power/weight | 311 hp/tonne |
| Length | 4,806 mm |

# Ford Shelby Mustang GT350R

Street-legal and track-ready, the GT350R is the mightiest Mustang in Ford's history. It is also powered by the most potent naturally-aspirated V8 Ford has ever made. Mated to the only transmission choice – a six-speed manual – the pony car gets to 60 mph in under four seconds, and the V8 revs to 8,250 rpm. Yee ha!

 **Performance**

| | |
|---|---|
| Top speed | 190 mph |
| 0–60 mph | 3.9 secs |
| Power | 533 hp |
| Torque | 713 Nm |

 **Engine**

| | |
|---|---|
| Capacity | 5.2-litre V8 |
| Type | Naturally aspirated |

 **Efficiency**

| | |
|---|---|
| Mileage | 14–21 mpg |

At 102 hp per litre, the V8 is Ford's most powerful naturally-aspirated road car engine ever. With R version's light weight – no rear seats and carbon-fibre wheels – acceleration is fierce.

 **Dimensions**

| | |
|---|---|
| Kerb weight | 1,658 kg |
| Power/weight | 321 hp/tonne |
| Length | 4,783 |

# BMW M4 CS

| Country of manufacture | Germany |

M cars are always special – and fast. But they are not always fast enough for everyone which is why BMW makes special-edition M cars. The breed began with the M3 Evolution in the 1980s and its successor is the M4 CS: lighter, more aerodynamic and more powerful – and able to lap the Nürburgring in 7 minutes 38 seconds.

Borrowing performance parts from the M4 GTS and the CLS , the CS (Club Sport) uses carbon fibre-reinforced plastic for bonnet, roof, rear diffuser and driveshaft . BMW has even thrown out moulded door handles and got natty

 **Performance**

| | |
|---|---|
| Top speed | 174 mph |
| 0–62 mph | 3.9 secs |
| Power | 460 hp |
| Torque | 600 Nm |

 **Engine**

| | |
|---|---|
| Capacity | 3.0-litre straight 6 |
| Type | Twin turbocharged |

 **Efficiency**

| | |
|---|---|
| Mileage | 34 mpg |

 **Dimensions**

| | |
|---|---|
| Kerb weight | 1,580 kg |
| Power/weight | 291 hp/tonne |

# Chevrolet Camaro ZL1

| Country of manufacture | United States |
|---|---|

Chevrolet was so confident of its new ZL1 it took it to Nürburgring for a few hot laps – with a very respectable 7 minutes 16 seconds result. The American muscle-car icon's supercharged 650 hp V8 can be had with a six-speed manual or 10-speed automatic. The latest model has lost weight and gained bigger Brembo brakes.

New aero features including a carbon-fibre rear wing, and air deflectors and dive planes on the front fascia produce grip-generating downforce to help the car stick harder and drive faster in the turns.

 **Performance**

| | |
|---|---|
| Top speed | 198 mph |
| 0–60 mph | 3.5 secs |
| Power | 650 hp |
| Torque | 881 Nm |

**Engine**

| | |
|---|---|
| Capacity | 6.2-litre V8 |
| Type | Supercharged |

**Efficiency**

| | |
|---|---|
| Mileage | 16–20 mpg |

**Dimensions**

| | |
|---|---|
| Kerb weight | 1,784 kg |
| Power/weight | 364 hp/tonne |
| Length | 4,783 mm |

# Mercedes-AMG GT R

**Country of manufacture** | **Germany**

Racing improves the breed, and for proof look no further than Mercedes' fastest coupe. The GT R is the most motorsport-influenced car they have ever made. GT3 influences extend to carbon body parts, Race Mode suspension setting, active rear steering, 585 hp and even Nürburgring 'Green Hell' paint colour!

The GT R's Panamericana grille – as once used on AMG road racers of old – has 15 vertical struts. On the GT R's rear, over the badge, sits a large static aerofoil.

 **Performance**

| | |
|---|---|
| Top speed | 198 mph |
| 0–62 mph | 3.6 secs |
| Power | 585 hp |
| Torque | 700 Nm |

 **Engine**

| | |
|---|---|
| Capacity | 4-litre V8 |
| Type | Twin turbocharged |

**Efficiency**

| | |
|---|---|
| Mileage | 24.8 mpg |

 **Dimensions**

| | |
|---|---|
| Kerb weight | 1,630 kg |
| Power/weight | 359 hp/tonne |
| Length | 4,551 mm |

# Porsche 911 Turbo S

| Country of manufacture | Germany |
| --- | --- |

Most cars are turbocharged these days but there's still only one Turbo: the 911 in its ultimate road specification. The wide-body 911 shape is familiar, but under the rear lid is almost 600 hp of turbocharged flat six, powering all four wheels for fantastic acceleration when you want it, and refined cruising when you don't.

The interior, like the smooth coupe body shape, still has plenty in common with the first 911 of 1963 – like the big rev counter behind the steering wheel. In Turbo S form it's got a lot more power though!

 **Performance**

| | |
| --- | --- |
| Top speed | 205 mph |
| 0–62 mph | 2.9 secs |
| Power | 580 hp |
| Torque | 750 Nm |

 **Engine**

| | |
| --- | --- |
| Capacity | 3.8-litre flat 6 |
| Type | Twin turbocharged |

**Efficiency**

| | |
| --- | --- |
| Mileage | 31 mpg |

 **Dimensions**

| | |
| --- | --- |
| Kerb weight | 1,675 kg |
| Power/weight | 346 hp/tonne |
| Length | 4,507 mm |

# Maserati GranTurismo MC Stradale

Classic name, classic looks and with its old-school naturally-aspirated 4.7-litre V8, classic engineering too – with the booming engine soundtrack to prove it! Though 10 years old now, the beautiful GranTurismo in its lightest and most powerful MC Stradale form is as evocative as fast Italian coupes come.

In the original MC Stradale – the racing version used in the Maserati Trofeo Championship – the back seats were ditched to save weight and make it go faster. In the later model, there's luxury for four passengers.

##  Performance

| | |
|---|---|
| Top speed | 188 mph |
| 0–62 mph | 4.5 secs |
| Power | 460 hp |
| Torque | 520 Nm |

##  Engine

| | |
|---|---|
| Capacity | 4.7-litre V8 |
| Type | Naturally aspirated |

##  Efficiency

| | |
|---|---|
| Mileage | 19.6 mpg |

##  Dimensions

| | |
|---|---|
| Kerb weight | 1,800 kg |
| Power/weight | 256 hp/tonne |
| Length | 4,933 mm |

# Sporting Sedans and Estates

▶ Meet the luxury sedans and estate that think they are sports cars! There is certainly nothing tame about these four-door saloons – and one five-door estate – when it comes to power and rocketship acceleration. Some have their top speeds limited to 155 mph but others max out at 190 or even 200 mph! And whether a gas-guzzling petrol V12 or clean battery-powered, all have one thing in common: plenty of room for all the family.

# Audi RS6 quattro

Audi defined the high performance estate with the RS2 of 1994 and the marque's four rings have been synonymous with the breed ever since. The latest RS6 is the ultimate all-wheel drive, all roads, all seasons everyday performance car. If the speed limiter is taken off, it'll do almost 190 mph.

A motoring writer described the RS6's interior as being 'built from granite made to look like plastic'. The interior, gets a high-performance makeover but is still fully functioning as a spacious and practical estate car.

 **Performance**

| | |
|---|---|
| Top speed | 155 mph |
| 0–62 mph | 3.7 secs |
| Power | 605 hp |
| Torque | 750 Nm |

**Engine**

| | |
|---|---|
| Capacity | 4.0-litre V8 |
| Type | Twin turbocharged |

 **Efficiency**

| | |
|---|---|
| Mileage | 29.4 mpg |

 **Dimensions**

| | |
|---|---|
| Kerb weight | 1,950 kg |
| Power/weight | 310 hp/tonne |
| Length | 4,979 mm |

# Jaguar XE SV Project 8

| Country of manufacture | United Kingdom |
|---|---|

Meet the most powerful road-going Jag of all time. The XE started life as a mild-mannered four-door, but after a visit to Jaguar's Special Vehicle Operations emerged as a fire-breathing monster. Its supercar performance is thanks to a supercharged V8 with 600 hp. The Track Pack version ditches the back seats to save weight.

Jaguar are making only 300 Project 8s – all left-hand drive – so they will be collector's items. While everything is dedicated to optimum performance, including F1-style silicon nitride ceramic wheel bearings, the cabin comforts have not been forgotten.

 **Performance**

| Top speed | 200 mph |
|---|---|
| 0–62 mph | 3.7 secs |
| Power | 600 hp |
| Torque | 700 Nm |

 **Engine**

| Capacity | 5.0-litre V8 |
|---|---|
| Type | Supercharged |

 **Efficiency**

| Mileage | Not available |
|---|---|

 **Dimensions**

| Curb weight | 1,745 kg |
|---|---|
| Power/weight | 344 hp/tonne |
| Length | 4,712 mm |

# BMW M760 Li V12

No four-door saloon over five metres long and 2.2 tonnes should be able to get from 0–62 mph in under four seconds. But the M760 Li can, and it is the German firm's flagship – a car in with a shout of being the world's greatest sporting limousine. It comes with Launch Control – so don't take it on in the traffic lights grand prix!

Perhaps the most techie car in its class. There's gesture control to change infotainment choice or volume, seats that massage you, and a key with touchscreen that will tell you fuel level and switch on preset heating. James Bond's Q would love it!

##  Performance

| | |
|---|---|
| Top speed | 155 mph |
| 0–62 mph | 3.7 secs |
| Power | 609 hp |
| Torque | 800 Nm |

##  Engine

| | |
|---|---|
| Capacity | 6.6-litre V12 |
| Type | Twin turbocharged |

##  Efficiency

| | |
|---|---|
| Mileage | 22.1 mpg |

##  Dimensions

| | |
|---|---|
| Kerb weight | 2,255 kg |
| Power/weight | 266 hp/tonne |

# Cadillac CTS-V

| Country of manufacture | United States |
|---|---|

The supercharged 6.2-litre V8 is performance currency in North America, but few cars use it as well as the CTS-V – four initials that sum up the very essence of 'supersedan'. The automatic rear-wheel drive car can blast to 200 mph, but with its sports suspension it's far more than a drag-strip special. It corners like a racer too!

The Carbon Black Package CTS-V has the power to stop as well as the power to go. Brakes are huge Brembo discs, six-piston at the rear. Wheels are huge too.

## Performance

| Top speed | 200 mph |
|---|---|
| 0–60 mph | 3.6 secs |
| Power | 640 hp |
| Torque | 854 Nm |

## Engine

| Capacity | 6.2-litre V8 |
|---|---|
| Type | Supercharged |

## Efficiency

| Mileage | 14–20 mpg |
|---|---|

## Dimensions

| Kerb weight | 1,878 kg |
|---|---|
| Power/weight | 341 hp/tonne |
| Length | 4,966 mm |

# Mercedes-AMG S65L

**untry of manufacture** | **Germany**

A Merc S-Class with the works goes by the name of AMG S65. To the awesome luxury and technology already in the world's favourite limo, AMG adds a sporting makeover including a twin-turbo V12 engine and 1,000 Nm of torque. Performance is totally effortless – and it's all as smooth and quiet as any S-Class!

The interior of the S65L is lit by about 300 LEDs – there's not a normal lighbulb anywhere! There are seven colour options and various lighting zones to dial up a lighting plan to suit your mood and needs.

## Performance

| | |
|---|---|
| Top speed | 155 mph |
| 0–62 mph | 4.3 secs |
| Power | 630 hp |
| Torque | 1,000 Nm |

## Engine

| | |
|---|---|
| Capacity | 6.0-litre V12 |
| Type | Twin turbocharged |

## Efficiency

| | |
|---|---|
| Mileage | 23.7 mpg |

## Dimensions

| | |
|---|---|
| Kerb weight | 2,250 kg |
| Power/weight | 280 hp/tonne |
| Length | 5,287 mm |

# Bentley Flying Spur W12 S

Bentley has been making fast cars since the 1920s, and winning Le Mans with them. But this ultimate Flying Spur takes things further – by being the first four-door Bentley to break the 200 mph barrier. Outside there are 21-inch wheels and carbon-ceramic brakes to make sure it slows down as fast as it accelerates!

The winged B says you have arrived, and in the W12 S you most probably got there darned fast! But for gentle exploring you might want options like the veneered picnic tables with vanity mirrors, bottle cooler and champagne flutes.

 **Performance**

| | |
|---|---|
| Top speed | 202 mph |
| 0–62 mph | 4.5 secs |
| Power | 635 hp |
| Torque | 820 Nm |

 **Engine**

| | |
|---|---|
| Capacity | 6.0-litre W12 |
| Type | Twin turbocharged |

**Efficiency**

| | |
|---|---|
| Mileage | 19.8 mpg |

 **Dimensions**

| | |
|---|---|
| Kerb weight | 2,475 kg |
| Power/weight | 257 hp/tonne |
| Length | 5,299 mm |

# Alfa Romeo Giulia 2.9 Quadrifoglio

**Country of manufacture** | **Italy**

At last, the famous Alfa Romeo badge is back on a performance saloon that really means business. The Quadrifoglio (it means four-leaf clover) gets 510 hp and pace scintillating enough to take on powerful German rivals. But it's also an Alfa, so it looks great, sounds great and has a distinct Italian character. *Ciao bella!*

The Alfa badge dates from 1910 when Alfa (Anonima Lombarda Fabbrica Automobili) started. The red cross represents Milan, which is Alfa's hometown. The snake spitting out a human stands for change and rebirth. There, now you know!

 **Performance**

| | |
|---|---|
| Top speed | 191 mph |
| 0–62 mph | 3.9 secs |
| Power | 510 hp |
| Torque | 600 Nm |

**Engine**

| | |
|---|---|
| Capacity | 2.9-litre V6 |
| Type | Twin turbocharged |

 **Efficiency**

| | |
|---|---|
| Mileage | 34.4 mpg |

 **Dimensions**

| | |
|---|---|
| Kerb weight | 1,524 kg |
| Power/weight | 335 hp/tonne |
| Length | 4,639 mm |

# 'esla Model S P100D 'Ludicrous'

**untry of manufacture | United States**

t's big, luxurious, all electric and ludicrously
fast, as the name of its sports driving mode
attests. Top speed is pegged back to 155 mph,
out on initial acceleration it's as fast as
Porsche's fastest sports car. The two-motor top
version Model S is in the record books for its
speed and will do over 300 miles on a charge.

## Performance

| | |
|---|---|
| Top speed | 155 mph |
| 0–60 mph | 2.7 secs |
| Power | 603 hp |
| Torque | 967 Nm |

## Engine

| | |
|---|---|
| Capacity | 100 kWh |
| Type | Plug-in electric |

## Efficiency

The Model S is the
world's top selling
electric car, and who
wouldn't want a car

# Aston Martin Rapide S

**Country of manufacture** | **United Kingdom**

If James Bond ever needs a family car here it is: Aston Martin's first four-door since the 1980s Lagonda. A stretched version of the superceded DB9, the Rapide looks, sounds and drives like an Aston Martin sports car, but with extra doors and rear seat room. Its V12 is pure Aston, but the future RapidE model will be all-electric!

To start the V12 in the Rapide you have to insert a large glass key in a slot on the dashboard. The engine sounds just as good as an Aston sports car – and this four-seater is almost as fast!

###  Performance

| | |
|---|---|
| Top speed | 203 mph |
| 0–62 mph | 4.4 secs |
| Power | 560 hp |
| Torque | 630 Nm |

###  Engine

| | |
|---|---|
| Capacity | 6.0-litre V12 |
| Type | Naturally aspirated |

###  Efficiency

| | |
|---|---|
| Mileage | 21.9 mpg |

###  Dimensions

| | |
|---|---|
| Kerb weight | 1,990 kg |
| Power/weight | 281 hp/tonne |
| Length | 5,019 mm |

# Porsche Panamera Turbo S E-Hybrid

| Country of manufacture | Germany |

Five-door hatchbacks don't come with any more impressive numbers than this plug-in petrol/electric Porsche. How does 97 mpg and 0–125 mph in just 11.7 secs sound? Plus there's room for four people and the dog! The secret is a combination of V8 and electric motor. It's mean and green and very, very keen.

Porsche has banned most of the buttons in the latest Panamera, now it's all touchscreen (12-in in the dash) and voice control. Very hi-tech – just like the car's hybrid drivetrain.

 **Performance**

| | |
|---|---|
| Top speed | 193 mph |
| 0–62 mph | 3.4 secs |
| Power | 680 hp |
| Torque | 850 Nm |

 **Engine**

| | |
|---|---|
| Capacity | 4.0-lire V8 |
| Type | Petrol/electric hybrid |

 **Efficiency**

| | |
|---|---|
| Mileage | 97 mpg |

 **Dimensions**

| | |
|---|---|
| Kerb weight | 2,385 kg |
| Power/weight | 285 hp/tonne |
| Length | 5,049 mm |

# Volvo S60 Polestar

**Country of manufacture** | **Sweden**

Polestar knows a lot about making safety-first Swedes get a move on: it has been racing Volvos for years. Now it's hotting up Volvos you can buy, and the S60 (and V60 estate) is its best yet – swift, rewarding, safe and efficient. Get it while you can: Polestar's future lies in an all-new range of high performance electric cars.

Volvos can be fast and satisfying too and none better than a Volvo that's had a makeover from Polestar. They are used to racing Volvos so know everything there is about making an S60 go fast!

##  Performance

| | |
|---|---|
| Top speed | 155 mph |
| 0–62 mph | 4.7 secs |
| Power | 367 hp |
| Torque | 470 Nm |

## Engine

| | |
|---|---|
| Capacity | 2.0-litre 4 cylinder |
| Type | Turbocharged and supercharged |

##  Efficiency

| | |
|---|---|
| Mileage | 29 mpg |

## Dimensions

| | |
|---|---|
| Kerb weight | 1,766 kg |
| Power/weight | 205 hp/tonne |
| Length | 4,635 mm |

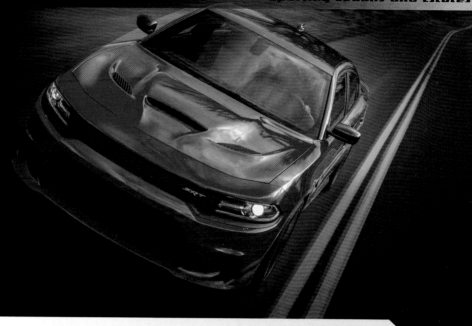

# Dodge SRT Hellcat Charger

**Country of manufacture** | **United States**

Claiming the title of world's most powerful production sedan, the Hellcat version of the four-door Charger has a massive 707 horses to propel it, enough even to keep its Cadillac CTS-V rival honest. In the two-door Challenger version you get 840 hp, and the fastest quarter-mile of any production car ever.

This family performance sedan with its sinister looks comes to a halt using the largest brakes ever offered in a Chrysler Group vehicle – 390-mm (15.4-inch) Brembo two-piece rotors with six-piston calipers.

##  Performance

| | |
|---|---|
| Top speed | 204 mph |
| 0–60 mph | 3.7 secs |
| Power | 707 hp |
| Torque | 881 Nm |

##  Engine

| | |
|---|---|
| Capacity | 6.2-litre V8 |
| Type | Supercharged |

## Efficiency

| | |
|---|---|
| Mileage | 13–22 mpg |

##  Dimensions

| | |
|---|---|
| Kerb weight | 2,075 kg |
| Power/weight | 341 hp/tonne |
| Length | 5,100 mm |

# Maserati Quattroporte GTS

The Maserati Four-Door – the name definitely sounds better in Italian – was the fastest four-door sedan in the world in the mid 1960s. In fact it was pretty much the only one, Maserati being first to combine a racing engine with a big saloon body. Now in its sixth generation, it comes with a Ferrari-derived V8 engine.

The cabin is swathed in the finest leather, the headrests are embossed with the Trident logo and there's plenty of room on sumptuous seats front and back. This Italian beauty comes with all the latest mod cons.

## Performance

| | |
|---|---|
| Top speed | 191 mph |
| 0–62 mph | 4.7 secs |
| Power | 530 hp |
| Torque | 710 Nm |

## Engine

| | |
|---|---|
| Capacity | 3.8-litre V8 |
| Type | Twin turbocharged |

## Efficiency

| | |
|---|---|
| Mileage | 26.4 mpg |

## Dimensions

| | |
|---|---|
| Kerb weight | 1,900 kg |
| Power/weight | 279 hp/tonne |
| Length | 5,262 mm |

# Holden Commodore HSV GTS-R W1

Say hello – and goodbye – to the greatest Aussie V8 muscle car ever...and also the last. It's GM Holden's most ferocious beast yet in a long line of high-performance Commodores. Available in the UK as a Vauxhall VXR8, the 'thunder from down under' in ultimate W1 version is a collector's edition.

The hot Aussie Commodore, along with all local production, ends in 2017 but it's bowing out in style with the W1 edition: this rear wing is all most people will ever see of it!

 **Performance**

| | |
|---|---|
| Top speed | 155 mph |
| 0–62 mph | 4.2 secs |
| Power | 644 hp |
| Torque | 815 Nm |

 **Engine**

| | |
|---|---|
| Capacity | 6.2-litre V8 |
| Type | Supercharged |

**Efficiency**

| | |
|---|---|
| Mileage | 17.1 mpg |

 **Dimensions**

| | |
|---|---|
| Kerb weight | 1,895 kg |
| Power/weight | 335 hp/tonne |
| Length | 5,044 mm |

# Convertibles

▶ Convertible, cabriolet, soft-top, ragtop, spider (and sometimes spyder) – whatever name you call them, cars without roofs open up a whole new world of high performance motoring. With the wind in your hair and the roar of the exhaust ringing in your ears, convertibles offer high-octane, high-profile thrills – especially when they are as fast as these babies...

# Jaguar F-Type SVR

| Country of manufacture | United Kingdom |
|---|---|

Like its spiritual forebear the E-Type, the F-Type comes in both coupe and cabriolet forms. Either car is quick in top of the range 575 hp SVR form, but opt for the convertible and top speed drops from the magic 200 mph to a mere 195! That's still a great deal faster than any E-Type. In fact it's the fastest Jag since the mighty XJ220.

The cat's aerodynamics include a carbon-fibre active rear wing and rear venturi to reduce lift and drag. And the bonus with the roof off: the uncensored soundtrack of V8 burble from the titanium pipes, with lots of pops and bangs when you change gear!

 **Performance**

| Top speed | 195 mph |
|---|---|
| 0–62 mph | 3.7 secs |
| Power | 575 hp |
| Torque | 700 Nm |

 **Engine**

| Capacity | 5.0-litre V8 |
|---|---|
| Type | Supercharged |

 **Efficiency**

| Mileage | 25.0 mpg |
|---|---|

 **Dimensions**

| Kerb weight | 1,720 kg |
|---|---|
| Power/weight | 334 hp/tonne |
| Length | 4,475 mm |

# Alfa Romeo 4C Spider

**untry of manufacture | Italy**

The 4C does what Alfas have always done best: go fast, look great and handle beautifully. The key to its scintillating pace is light weight and a giant turbocharger, which together make its small 1.7-litre engine feel (and sound!) far gruntier than its 240 hp would suggest. With 0–62 mph in 4.5 secs it's a visceral experience.

The much disliked ugly bug-eye lights that marred the front of the earlier model have been replaced with traditional headlamps. Now that's sorted, pundits can talk about just how beautiful this Alfa really is.

 **Performance**

| | |
|---|---|
| Top speed | 160 mph |
| 0–62 mph | 4.5 secs |
| Power | 240 hp |
| Torque | 350 Nm |

 **Engine**

| | |
|---|---|
| Capacity | 1.7-litre 4 cylinder |
| Type | Turbocharged |

**Efficiency**

| | |
|---|---|
| Mileage | 40.9 mpg |

 **Dimensions**

| | |
|---|---|
| Curb weight | 999 kg |
| Power/weight | 240 hp/tonne |
| Length | 3,990 mm |

# BMW M240i

**Country of manufacture** | **Germany**

There's no M2 convertible (yet) but there is the M240i cabriolet. And it's almost as good! Small, agile and immensely chuckable, there's nothing not to like in this 340-hp baby bombshell that can sprint from rest to 62 mph in just five seconds. Plus there are seats in the back, so you get to share the thrills with friends.

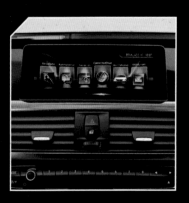

If the M240i's performance doesn't make you app-y, its user-friendly connectivity will. All your favourite apps appear on the new-look dashboard.

## Performance

| | |
|---|---|
| Top speed | 155 mph |
| 0–62 mph | 5.0 secs |
| Power | 340 hp |
| Torque | 500 Nm |

## Engine

| | |
|---|---|
| Capacity | 3.0-litre straight 6 |
| Type | Turbocharged |

## Efficiency

| | |
|---|---|
| Mileage | 34 mpg |

## Dimensions

| | |
|---|---|
| Kerb weight | 1,690 kg |
| Power/weight | 202 hp/tonne |
| Length | 4,454 mm |

# Aston Martin V12 Vantage

**Country of manufacture** | **United Kingdom**

Vantage is a famous Aston Martin name reserved for its fastest cars, and this specimen doesn't disappoint. It might be Aston's oldest model (dating to 2005) but with 0–62 mph in 3.9 seconds it's as fast as the 2017 DB11! Originally a V8 coupe, the top spec today is the hand-built convertible body with V12 under the bonnet.

Aston's un-turbocharged V12 is old-school and all the better for it: it is one of the best-sounding engines in production. This car has pure charisma, along with storming performance.

 **Performance**

| | |
|---|---|
| Top speed | 201 mph |
| 0–62 mph | 3.9 secs |
| Power | 573 hp |
| Torque | 620 Nm |

 **Engine**

| | |
|---|---|
| Capacity | 6.0-litre V12 |
| Type | Naturally aspirated |

 **Efficiency**

| | |
|---|---|
| Mileage | 19.2 mpg |

 **Dimensions**

| | |
|---|---|
| Kerb weight | 1,665 kg |
| Power/weight | 344 hp/tonne |
| Length | 4,385 mm |

# Mazda MX-5

**Country of manufacture** | Japan

The world's favourite sports car was a hit the day it arrived in 1989 and, four model generations later, it's still as popular. The MX-5 has never been the most powerful or fastest car in the world, but it has always been one of the most fun to drive, doing really well those things that old British sports cars did badly!

The designers/engineers at Mazda are all about *Jinba Ittai*, which is the unity of car and driver – yes, even when it comes to having somewhere to put your coffee! But car/driver unity shows up most of all in how sweet the MX-5 is to drive.

 **Performance**

| | |
|---|---|
| Top speed | 133 mph |
| 0–62 mph | 7.3 secs |
| Power | 160 hp |
| Torque | 200 Nm |

 **Engine**

| | |
|---|---|
| Capacity | 2.0-litre 4 cylinder |
| Type | Naturally aspirated |

 **Efficiency**

| | |
|---|---|
| Mileage | 47.1 mpg |

 **Dimensions**

| | |
|---|---|
| Kerb weight | 1,075 kg |
| Power/weight | 149 hp/tonne |
| Length | 3,915 mm |

# Fiat Abarth 124

The Fiat 124 Spider was one of the most popular 1960s sports cars. Now it's back, and in Abarth form! It shares vehicle architecture with the Mazda MX-5 but that hasn't stopped the Italians making it look super-cool, with its thrusting nose (like the Pininfarina original), bonnet power bulges and racy paint job.

This car's controls shout *guida sportiva* (sporty drive) in true Italian tradition. The small diameter steering wheel (with red centre mark), big rev counter, grippy seats and well-spaced pedals all say: drive me!

 **Performance**

| Top speed | 144 mph |
|---|---|
| 0–62 mph | 6.8 secs |
| Power | 170 hp |
| Torque | 250 Nm |

 **Engine**

| Capacity | 1.4-litre 4 cylinder |
|---|---|
| Type | Turbocharged |

 **Efficiency**

| Mileage | 44.1 mpg |
|---|---|

 **Dimensions**

| Kerb weight | 1,060 kg |
|---|---|
| Power/weight | 160 hp/tonne |
| Length | 4,054 mm |

# Porsche 718 Boxster S

| Country of manufacture | Germany |
| --- | --- |

It's wind-in-the-hair thrills with the 177-mph, mid-engined, two-seat Boxster in sporty S form. The '718' in its badge revives the name of an old Porsche racing car. Like all Boxsters it has a 'boxer' engine with horizontally-opposed cylinders, but since 2016 it's a four-cylinder turbo – even Porsches must downsize!

The Boxster has always had a generous rear end (there's an engine under that flat rear deck), but in latest 718 form it looks sharper. In the corners, the handling is sharp too!

## Performance

| | |
| --- | --- |
| Top speed | 177 mph |
| 0–62 mph | 4.6 secs |
| Power | 350 hp |
| Torque | 420 Nm |

## Engine

| | |
| --- | --- |
| Capacity | 2.5-litre flat 4 |
| Type | Turbocharged |

## Efficiency

| | |
| --- | --- |
| Mileage | 34.9 mpg |

## Dimensions

| | |
| --- | --- |
| Kerb weight | 1,430 kg |
| Power/weight | 245 hp/tonne |
| Length | 4,379 mm |

# Mercedes-AMG SL65

**Country of manufacture** | **Germany**

The Mercedes SL has an honourable history on road and track. Today, SL is a byword for the most hi-tech and civilized convertible motoring on the planet. But in AMG SL65 form, that doesn't mean slow. This monster SL's top speed is limited, but 0–62 mph in 4.0 secs shows this mighty Merc's true performance colours.

Not only does this glam Merc have 12 cylinders, its Bang & Olufsen audio system blasts out 900 watts of power through 12 speakers. All the better for you and anyone in a five-kilometre radius to hear.

## Performance

| | |
|---|---|
| Top speed | 155 mph |
| 0–62 mph | 4.0 secs |
| Power | 630 hp |
| Torque | 1,000 Nm |

## Engine

| | |
|---|---|
| Capacity | 6.0-litre V12 |
| Type | Twin turbocharged |

## Efficiency

| | |
|---|---|
| Mileage | 23.7 mpg |

## Dimensions

| | |
|---|---|
| Kerb weight | 1,950 kg |
| Power/weight | 323 hp/tonne |
| Length | 4,631 mm |

# Morgan Aero 8

**Country of manufacture** | **United Kingdom**

With its old-school looks it could only be that unique phenomenon that is a Morgan motor car. But as well as being 170 mph fast, this is a very modern Morgan – there's no wooden body frame and under the long bonnet is a BMW 4.8-litre V8. With the top down and the exhaust booming, country cruising was never better!

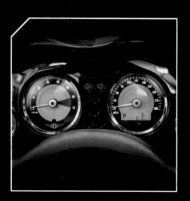

It's a Morgan, so what else but a wood dashboard and big dials? But in the Aero 8 tradition goes hand in hand with hi-tech, as well as a great deal of power courtesy of a BMW V8.

## Performance

| | |
|---|---|
| Top speed | 170 mph |
| 0–62 mph | 4.5 secs |
| Power | 367 hp |
| Torque | 490 Nm |

## Engine

| | |
|---|---|
| Capacity | 4.8-litre V8 |
| Type | Naturally aspirated |

## Efficiency

| | |
|---|---|
| Mileage | 23.3 mpg |

## Dimensions

| | |
|---|---|
| Kerb weight | 1,180 kg |
| Power/weight | 311 hp/tonne |
| Length | 4,147 mm |

# Lamborghini Huracan LP610-4

**Country of manufacture** | **Italy**

Lamborghini invented the supercar 50 years ago with the Miura, and as the Huracan shows they've not lost their touch. It's the epitome of contemporary cool. The Spyder version of the 200-mph LP610-4 (610 is hp, 4 for all-wheel drive) is the best way of hearing a naturally-aspirated V10 screaming to 8,250 rpm!

Top down, V10 burbling, this is surely the only way to arrive on the Italian Riviera! With a cockpit like this, the drive there would be pure unbridled pleasure.

 **Performance**

| | |
|---|---|
| Top speed | 201 mph |
| 0–62 mph | 3.4 secs |
| Power | 610 hp |
| Torque | 560 Nm |

 **Engine**

| | |
|---|---|
| Capacity | 5.2-litre V10 |
| Type | Naturally aspirated |

**Efficiency**

| | |
|---|---|
| Mileage | 22.6 mpg |

 **Dimensions**

| | |
|---|---|
| Kerb weight | 1,420 kg |
| Power/weight | 430 hp/tonne |
| Length | 4,459 mm |

# Chevrolet Corvette Z07

| Country of manufacture | United States |
| --- | --- |

The legend of America's only true sports car continues! Any of the new (seventh-generation) Corvette family, which resurrected the Stingray name, is a powerhouse of performance and styling. But in 6.2-litre supercharged Z06 form – and ideally fitted with the Z07 Performance Pack – it's a world-class contender.

The Z07 package adds adjustable aero components, like the front winglets for convincing downforce, Michelin Pilot Super Sport Cup tyres for top grip and Brembo carbon ceramic brake rotors.

###  Performance

| | |
| --- | --- |
| Top speed | 205 mph |
| 0–60 mph | 2.9 secs |
| Power | 650 hp |
| Torque | 881 Nm |

### Engine

| | |
| --- | --- |
| Capacity | 6.2-litre V8 |
| Type | Supercharged |

### Efficiency

| | |
| --- | --- |
| Mileage | 15–22 mpg |

### Dimensions

| | |
| --- | --- |
| Kerb weight | 1,598 kg |
| Power/weight | 407 hp/tonne |
| Length | 4,519 mm |

# Lotus Elise Cup 250

| **Country of manufacture** | **United Kingdom** |

The Elise has been delighting boy (and girl) racers for years, and with each new version it gets a little lighter, a little more powerful and a whole lot more fun to drive. This new Cup 250 is the fastest Elise to date. Its supercharged 1.8-litre engine delivers 243 hp that lets it sprint to 62 mph from standstill in sub four seconds!

The latest version of the Elise Cup 250 is a lightweight in every respect – except its performance. The boffins in Norfolk, UK, have 'added lightness' by using carbon fibre, titanium and aluminium. If it ain't needed, it ain't on the car!

 **Performance**

| Top speed | 154 mph |
|---|---|
| 0–62 mph | 3.9 secs |
| Power | 243 hp |
| Torque | 250 Nm |

 **Engine**

| Capacity | 1.8-litre 4 cylinder |
|---|---|
| Type | Supercharged |

 **Efficiency**

| Mileage | 37.7 mpg |
|---|---|

 **Dimensions**

| Kerb weight | 931 kg |
|---|---|
| Power/weight | 261 hp/tonne |
| Length | 3,824 mm |

# *Supercars*

▶ Impossibly low, sleek and fast-looking even when standing still, supercars are the poster stars of the motoring world. Photographs of them in exotic locations have adorned bedroom walls for generations, ever since the blueprint for the first modern supercars was established in the 1960s. Today there's more choice than ever from more supercar companies than ever, all using a vast array of new technologies. But some things never change: they are faster than ever and all still drop-dead gorgeous to look at.

# Honda/Acura NSX

**Country of manufacture** | **United States**

The sleek NSX is a technological *tour de force* from the makers of the Civic hatchback! With a V6, three electric motors and all-wheel drive it's fast and surefooted, but easy to drive. The first NSX (1991) remade the supercar as something you could use every day, a tradition the new model takes into the supercar stratosphere.

Interwoven under the leather dash panel is the exposed mid-frame – a functioning chassis member like those on a naked sport bike. An ultra-thin A-pillar and low-mounted instrument panel maximize the driver's view of the road.

 **Performance**

| | |
|---|---|
| Top speed | 191 mph |
| 0–62 mph | 3.3 secs |
| Power | 581 hp |
| Torque | 645 Nm |

**Engine**

| | |
|---|---|
| Capacity | 3.5-litre V6 |
| Type | Petrol/electric hybrid |

 **Efficiency**

| | |
|---|---|
| Mileage | 28.2 mpg |

 **Dimensions**

| | |
|---|---|
| Kerb weight | 1,776 kg |
| Power/weight | 327 hp/tonne |
| Length | 4,487 mm |

# Dodge Viper

The all-American Viper is the supercar they couldn't kill! The V10-powered two-seater has been around in one form or another since 1992 but people just love it so much new ones are still hot. And the Viper for 2017 – sadly, its final year – is doubly hot. It's bowing out in style: faster, louder and more brash than ever.

Over eight litres of V10 engine is not for the faint-hearted! Watch those revs or this Viper will bite – one reason the latest (and last) version comes with electronic stability control.

## Performance

| | |
|---|---|
| Top speed | 206 mph |
| 0–62 mph | 3.4 secs |
| Power | 645 hp |
| Torque | 813 Nm |

## Engine

| | |
|---|---|
| Capacity | 8.4-litre V10 |
| Type | Naturally aspirated |

## Efficiency

| | |
|---|---|
| Mileage | 12–19 mpg |

## Dimensions

| | |
|---|---|
| Kerb weight | 1,532 kg |
| Power/weight | 421 hp/tonne |
| Length | 4,463 mm |

# BMW i8

Way ahead of its time when launched, the i8 is a plug-in hybrid with a tiny three-cylinder engine at the back and a big electric motor up front, with batteries under the cabin floor. Its looks are as progressive as the technology, and its figures astonishing: 0–62 mph in 4.4 secs and 134 mpg, and up to 75 mph on electric alone.

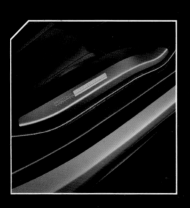

In the special edition Frozen Yellow i8 the door sill finisher declares its exclusive status, and in the cabin the seats have yellow stitching and the headrests are embossed with the i8 logo. This car's so good, you'll never let it go!

 **Performance**

| | |
|---|---|
| Top speed | 155 mph |
| 0–62 mph | 4.4 secs |
| Power | 362 hp |
| Torque | 570 Nm |

 **Engine**

| | |
|---|---|
| Capacity | 1.5-litre 3 cylinder |
| Type | Petrol/electric hybrid |

 **Efficiency**

| | |
|---|---|
| Mileage | 134.5 mpg |

 **Dimensions**

| | |
|---|---|
| Kerb weight | 1,560 kg |
| Power/weight | 232 hp/tonne |
| Length | 4,689 mm |

# Ford GT

| Country of manufacture | Canada |
|---|---|

The fastest-ever Ford is a thinly disguised racing car for the road! In that it is just like its ancestor, the iconic 1960s GT40. It has even followed in the GT40's tyre tracks by winning at Le Mans. A true Ferrari/McLaren rival, the GT boasts massive power from the turbocharged V6, an incredible top speed and stunning looks.

Only 500 Ford GTs are being made, and they are all sold. But if you did have one, this is what you would see on its 10-in digital display when the GT hit its top speed of 216 mph.

##  Performance

| Top speed | 216 mph |
|---|---|
| 0–62 mph | 2.9 secs (estimate) |
| Power | 655 hp |
| Torque | 746 Nm |

## Engine

| Capacity | 3.5-litre V6 |
|---|---|
| Type | Twin turbocharged |

##  Efficiency

| Mileage | 16.8 mpg |
|---|---|

##  Dimensions

| Kerb weight | 1,385 kg |
|---|---|
| Power/weight | 473 hp/tonne |
| Length | 4,763 mm |

# Lamborghini Aventador Superveloce

**Country of manufacture** | **Italy**

No one does ferocious speed and outlandish looks better than Lamborghini. And the Aventador Superveloce (super-fast) is a poster-car in the mould of greats like the Countach. Named after a fighting bull, the flagship supercar's V12 is mounted behind the seats. Power? 740 hp! And it's not even turbocharged!

Centre stacks don't come much wider than this. It's a real button-fest. Black trim and yellow piping are very Lambo, as is the rev counter dominating the instrument binnacle.

 **Performance**

| | |
|---|---|
| Top speed | 217 mph |
| 0–62 mph | 2.9 secs |
| Power | 740 hp |
| Torque | 690 Nm |

**Engine**

| | |
|---|---|
| Capacity | 6.5-litre V12 |
| Type | Naturally aspirated |

 **Efficiency**

| | |
|---|---|
| Mileage | 16.7 mpg |

 **Dimensions**

| | |
|---|---|
| Kerb weight | 1,575 kg |
| Power/weight | 470 hp/tonne |
| Length | 4,797 mm |

# Porsche 911 GT2 RS

| Country of manufacture | Germany |
|---|---|

It's the ultimate 911! Never before has Porsche's iconic sports car been this powerful and driver focused. It debuted at the Goodwood Festival of Speed in 2017, and speed is this car's middle name. It is two-wheel drive but has four-wheel steering for extra agility, and there's a Weissach handling pack option for really serious drivers.

Not fast enough for you? You need the Weissach pack. It replaces key components – like the roof – with carbon fibre to save weight. You can even get a roll cage made of…titanium!

 **Performance**

| | |
|---|---|
| Top speed | 211 mph |
| 0–62 mph | 2.8 secs |
| Power | 700 hp |
| Torque | 750 Nm |

 **Engine**

| | |
|---|---|
| Capacity | 3.8-litre flat 6 |
| Type | Twin turbocharged |

 **Efficiency**

| | |
|---|---|
| Mileage | 24 mpg |

 **Dimensions**

| | |
|---|---|
| Kerb weight | 1,470 kg |
| Power/weight | 476 hp/tonne |
| Length | 4,545 mm |

# Audi R8 V10 Plus

**Country of manufacture** | **Germany**

Supercars don't come more user-friendly than the R8 – here's a 205-mph car your gran could drive! That doesn't mean it is boring. Audi has avoided turbocharging its V10 with the result that it is powerful and revs to past 8,000 rpm, but sounds majestic. There's a special button to push to make the exhaust sound even louder!

Twenty-four R8 V10 Plus 'selection 24h' models will be built, combining competition-inspired styling enhancements, including a sport exhaust for further amplification of the R8's much-loved 10-cylinder soundtrack.

 **Performance**

| | |
|---|---|
| Top speed | 205 mph |
| 0–62 mph | 3.2 secs |
| Power | 610 hp |
| Torque | 560 Nm |

 **Engine**

| | |
|---|---|
| Capacity | 5.2-litre V10 |
| Type | Naturally aspirated |

☑ **Efficiency**

| | |
|---|---|
| Mileage | 23.0 mpg |

 **Dimensions**

| | |
|---|---|
| Kerb weight | 1,555 kg |
| Power/weight | 392 hp/tonne |
| Length | 4,426 mm |

# Spyker C8 Preliator

**Country of manufacture** | **United Kingdom**

Preliator – it means warrior – is everything a Spyker should be: advanced, individual and inspired by airplanes. Spyker is a Dutch brand with an aviation heritage, but known since 2000 as a supercar manufacturer. The latest C8 Preliator has a mighty Koenigsegg engine! It is one of few 600-hp cars with a manual gearbox.

Much of the C8's design is heavily inspired by Spyker's aviation heritage, but the Latin motto pressed into the exhaust is very down to earth: for the tenacious, no road is impassable.

 **Performance**

| | |
|---|---|
| Top speed | 201 mph |
| 0–62 mph | 3.6 secs |
| Power | 600 hp |
| Torque | 600 Nm |

 **Engine**

| | |
|---|---|
| Capacity | 5.0-litre V8 |
| Type | Naturally aspirated |

 **Efficiency**

| | |
|---|---|
| Mileage | Not available |

 **Dimensions**

| | |
|---|---|
| Kerb weight | 1,390 kg |
| Power/weight | 432 hp/tonne |
| Length | 4,628 mm |

# McLaren 720S

Britain's supercar success gets better and better. And the cars keep getting faster! New for 2017, the 720S is the first of a new range of Super Series cars that began with the 2011 12C. It is a break with what went before in many ways, including its design and aerodynamics, said to offer twice the downforce of its predecessor.

Some earlier McLarens were a bit tricky to actually get into, but no contortions are required to slip into the 720S's cabin through its twin-hinged dihedral doors. Once in, get comfy and buckle up for the 212-mph ride of your life.

 **Performance**

| Top speed | 212 mph |
|---|---|
| 0–62 mph | 2.9 secs |
| Power | 720 hp |
| Torque | 770 Nm |

 **Engine**

| Capacity | 4.0-litre V8 |
|---|---|
| Type | Twin turbocharged |

**Efficiency**

| Mileage | 26.4 mpg |
|---|---|

 **Dimensions**

| Kerb weight | 1,419 kg |
|---|---|
| Power/weight | 507 hp/tonne |
| Length | 4,543 mm |

# Lotus Exige Sport 380

| Country of manufacture | United Kingdom |
| --- | --- |

More power, less weight and more aerodynamic downforce – that's the Lotus way. Few cars exemplify that as well as the firm's fastest model, the Exige Sport 380, 'the supercar killer'. With 0–62 mph in 3.7 secs, it is as fast as some supercars with twice the Lotus's power. Carbon fibre seats is one of its weight-saving tricks.

Small winglets at the car's sides help increase downforce while there's also a carbon front splitter and rear diffuser to reduce pressure under the car – all very F1!

## Performance

| | |
| --- | --- |
| Top speed | 170 mph |
| 0–62 mph | 3.7 secs |
| Power | 380 hp |
| Torque | 410 Nm |

## Engine

| | |
| --- | --- |
| Capacity | 3.5-litre V6 |
| Type | Supercharged |

## Efficiency

| | |
| --- | --- |
| Mileage | 27.2 mpg |

## Dimensions

| | |
| --- | --- |
| Kerb weight | 1,100 kg |
| Power/weight | 345 hp/tonne |
| Length | 4,084 mm |

# Ferrari 488 GTB

**Country of manufacture** | **Italy**

The 488 GTB is the latest in a distinguished line of mid-engined two-seaters with beautiful curves. These have usually been courtesy of designers Pininfarina, but Ferrari did the 488 themselves. It's different in other ways too – it is the first GTB to have a turbocharged engine. It doesn't slow it down any though!

Leather dash with contrast stiching, Ferrari red rev counter, a steering wheel that says 'hold me' and a big red 'Start' button – what more could you want?

### Performance

| | |
|---|---|
| Top speed | 205 mph |
| 0–62 mph | 3.0 secs |
| Power | 670 hp |
| Torque | 760 Nm |

### Engine

| | |
|---|---|
| Capacity | 3.9-litre V8 |
| Type | Twin turbocharged |

### Efficiency

| | |
|---|---|
| Mileage | 24.8 mpg |

### Dimensions

| | |
|---|---|
| Kerb weight | 1,475 kg |
| Power/weight | 454 hp/tonne |
| Length | 4,568 mm |

# Aston Martin Vanquish S

James Bond would approve! The latest Vanquish S is surely his sort of car. Sitting atop Aston Martin's range, the 2016-revised S looks more assertive than ever with its new carbon-fibre front splitter and rear diffuser. The V12 has been tuned to give 600 hp and has the best exhaust roar in all of motoring.

The Vanquish S is just as stunning on the inside as it is from kerbside. Carbon fibre isn't just the material of choice, it is at the heart of the styling. Ever seen a centre console like this before?

## Performance

| | |
|---|---|
| Top speed | 201 mph |
| 0–62 mph | 3.5 secs |
| Power | 600 hp |
| Torque | 630 Nm |

## Engine

| | |
|---|---|
| Capacity | 6.0-litre V12 |
| Type | Naturally aspirated |

## Efficiency

| | |
|---|---|
| Mileage | 21.6 mpg |

## Dimensions

| | |
|---|---|
| Kerb weight | 1,739 kg |
| Power/weight | 345 hp/tonne |
| Length | 4,730 mm |

# Hypercars

▶ Supercars used to be the ultimate four-wheeled machines but today there is a new breed at the very pinnacle of the performance spectrum – hypercars. So extreme are they that their closest rivals are pure racing cars. Like Formula 1 cars, the key to their other-worldly performance is the latest technology, with many turning to energy recovery systems (ERS) and hybrid or all-electric drivetrains to offer the most incredible speed, while active aerodynamics ensures never-before-achieved cornering abilities. Hypercars are the ultimate head-turners – with the ultimate price tags!

Fernando ALONSO

# Pagani Huayra BC

| Country of manufacture | Italy |

Italian works of supercar art are rarely as beautifully crafted or ferociously fast as a Pagani. First was the Zonda then came the Huayra (*wire-ah*) that the Stig set a *Top Gear* track record with. Now there's the Huayra BC, a road car for maximum track fun, powered by a huge AMG engine with a mighty V12 roar.

The Huayra BC – the initials stand for Benny Caiola, the first person to buy a Pagani – gets a titanium exhaust that would look at home in an art gallery. The exhaust weighs just 2.9 kg.

### Performance

| | |
|---|---|
| Top speed | 238 mph |
| 0–62 mph | 2.8 secs |
| Power | 780 hp |
| Torque | 1,100 Nm |

### Engine

| | |
|---|---|
| Capacity | 6.0-litre V12 |
| Type | Twin turbocharged |

### Efficiency

| | |
|---|---|
| Mileage | Not available |

### Dimensions

| | |
|---|---|
| Kerb weight | 1,218 kg |
| Power/weight | 640 hp/tonne |
| Length | 4,605 mm |

# Porsche 918 Spyder

**ountry of manufacture** | **Germany**

The 918 Spyder is one of the cars that wrote the hypercar rulebook when it arrived in 2013. A plug-in hybrid, its V8 is supplemented by two electric motors. Heavier and not as powerful as LaFerrari or McLaren P1, it is as fast thanks to awesome torque and all-wheel drive traction. Plus it can do city runs on battery power alone!

The 918 cars Porsche made of the 918 sold out in just a year. To choose one of the five operating modes – Race, Sport, E, E-Power and Hybrid – there's a motorsport-type 'map switch' on the steering wheel so the driver's attention stays on the road.

 **Performance**

| | |
|---|---|
| Top speed | 214 mph |
| 0–62 mph | 2.6 secs |
| Power | 887 hp |
| Torque | 1,280 Nm |

 **Engine**

| | |
|---|---|
| Capacity | 4.6-litre V8 |
| Type | Petrol/electric hybrid |

 **Efficiency**

| | |
|---|---|
| Mileage | 91.1 mpg |

 **Dimensions**

| | |
|---|---|
| Kerb weight | 1,640 kg |
| Power/weight | 541 hp/tonne |
| Length | 4,643 mm |

# Koenigsegg One:1

**Country of manufacture** | **Sweden**

Meet the world's first megacar! That's a car with one whole megawatt of power – in fact just over it, at 1,360 hp, in order to match the 1,360 kg weight and achieve the hypercar holy grail of a 1:1 power/weight ratio. One 2015 performance benchmark is mind-boggling: 0–200 mph in 14.3 secs – and back to nought again in just 6.0 secs!

A real Swedish stormer, and stunning to boot. Assembling the body shell from 400 separate pieces takes 600 hours. Just painting a car takes between 800 and 1,200 hours, depending on the final finish.

 **Performance**

| | |
|---|---|
| Top speed | 250 mph (estimate) |
| 0–62 mph | 2.8 secs |
| Power | 1,360 hp |
| Torque | 1,371 Nm |

 **Engine**

| | |
|---|---|
| Capacity | 5.0-litre V8 |
| Type | Twin turbocharged |

**Efficiency**

| | |
|---|---|
| Mileage | Not available |

 **Dimensions**

| | |
|---|---|
| Kerb weight | 1,360 kg |
| Power/weight | 1,000 hp/tonne |
| Length | 4,500 mm |

# Zenvo TS1 GT

**Country of manufacture** | **Denmark**

Danish manufacturer Zenvo celebrated its first decade in 2017 with a special TS1 GT Tenth Anniversary model. Named 'Sleipnir' after a Norse king's very fast eight-legged horse, it is painted Fjord Blue with copper-bronze strips set into the bare carbon-fibre hood and roof. Like all TS1s it is stunning and immensely powerful.

Each hand-made Anniversary model interior takes 8,000 man hours, with the copper and rhodium in the cabin switchgear costing the same as a Porsche 911!

 **Performance**

| | |
|---|---|
| Top speed | 233 mph |
| 0–62 mph | 2.8 secs |
| Power | 1,180 hp |
| Torque | 1,100 Nm |

 **Engine**

| | |
|---|---|
| Capacity | 5.8-litre V8 |
| Type | Twin supercharger |

 **Efficiency**

| | |
|---|---|
| Mileage | Not available |

 **Dimensions**

| | |
|---|---|
| Kerb weight | 1,710 kg |
| Power/weight | 690 hp/tonne |
| Length | 4,680 mm |

# Hennessey Venom GT

Here's a real rocketship! The Venom GT's world's fastest car claim dates from 2014 and its 270.49 mph achieved on the Space Shuttle runway at NASA's Kennedy Space Center. Another car to claim the magic 1:1 ratio, 12 of the Bugatti-beaters have been built since 2010. Next up: a Venom F5 with 300 mph targeted!

Built as both coupes and spyders, the first spyder was built for Steve Tyler from the band Aerosmith. The final edition, finished in glacier blue with white stripes, rolled out of the factory on January 17, 2017 to some lucky lead-foot collector.

 **Performance**

| | |
|---|---|
| Top speed | 270 mph |
| 0–60 mph | 2.7 secs |
| Power | 1,244 hp |
| Torque | 1,566 Nm |

 **Engine**

| | |
|---|---|
| Capacity | 7.0-litre V8 |
| Type | Twin turbocharged |

**Efficiency**

| | |
|---|---|
| Mileage | Not available |

 **Dimensions**

| | |
|---|---|
| Kerb weight | 1,244 kg |
| Power/weight | 1,000 hp/tonne |
| Length | 4,655 mm |

# Bugatti Chiron

| Country of manufacture | France |

How to replace a car like the Veyron? Easy, make it lighter and a lot more powerful! With another 500 hp over its record-breaking forebear, the Chiron will get from 0–124 mph in 6.5 secs. You need a special key to unleash its top speed, and even then at 261 mph it has been artificially held back for safety reasons.

Chiron's speedo is a record-breaker: it's the first to read all the way to 500 kph (310 mph). The exquisite cabin is a beautiful place from which to experience unbridled speed. Just 500 Chirons are being made.

### Performance

| | |
|---|---|
| Top speed | 261 mph |
| 0–62 mph | 2.5 secs |
| Power | 1,500 hp |
| Torque | 1,600 Nm |

### Engine

| | |
|---|---|
| Capacity | 8.0-litre W16 |
| Type | Quad turbocharged |

### Efficiency

| | |
|---|---|
| Mileage | 22.5 mpg |

### Dimensions

| | |
|---|---|
| Kerb weight | 1,995 kg |
| Power/weight | 752 hp/tonne |
| Length | 4,544 mm |

# Ferrari LaFerrari

| Country of manufacture | Italy |

The ultimate Ferrari is THE Ferrari, hence the name! It's certainly the most powerful and fastest, with its mild hybrid kinetic energy recovery system (KERS) providing an F1-style performance boost. The 499 coupes sold out as soon as the car was unveiled – with a special 500th car selling at auction for US$7 million.

The most valuable new car of the 21st century, the cockpit design layout of the LaFerrari was done in consultation with Fernando Alonso and Felipe Massa. The seat, which is modelled to the driver, is fixed in place but steering wheel and pedals are adjustable.

 **Performance**

| | |
|---|---|
| Top speed | 217 mph |
| 0–62 mph | Sub 3.0 secs |
| Power | 963 hp |
| Torque | 900 Nm |

 **Engine**

| | |
|---|---|
| Capacity | 6.3-litre V12 |
| Type | Petrol/electric hybrid |

 **Efficiency**

| | |
|---|---|
| Mileage | 20.2 mpg |

 **Dimensions**

| | |
|---|---|
| Kerb weight | 1,585 kg |
| Power/weight | 608 hp/tonne |
| Length | 4,702 mm |

# McLaren P1

| Country of manufacture | United Kingdom |
|---|---|

Britain's hypercar hero since 2014, McLaren's 'Ultimate Series' car is much lighter than its Porsche and Ferrari rivals. That, along with its twin-turbo V8/electric motor and active aerodynamics, gives it scintillating circuit pace. A road version of the P1 GTR has become the fastest road-registerable car at the Nürburgring.

In a race at Silverstone, the British, German and Italian hypercars finished within 0.5 secs of each other – with the P1 first. Most appropriate as P1, inspired by F1, refers to first place. McLaren itself refers to the automaker's original founder, Bruce McLaren.

 **Performance**

| | |
|---|---|
| Top speed | 217 mph |
| 0–62 mph | 2.8 secs |
| Power | 916 hp |
| Torque | 980 Nm |

 **Engine**

| | |
|---|---|
| Capacity | 3.8-litre V8 |
| Type | Petrol/electric hybrid |

**Efficiency**

| | |
|---|---|
| Mileage | 34.0 mpg |

**Dimensions**

| | |
|---|---|
| Kerb weight | 1,395 kg |
| Power/weight | 657 hp/tonne |
| Length | 4,588 mm |

# Techrules Ren

| Country of manufacture | China |
|---|---|

Chinese ingenuity meets Italian design drama in the Ren, one of the wildest hypercars yet. The electric three-seater, with its lift-up canopy like a fighter jet's, uses a small diesel turbine to charge the batteries. Techrules says it can go for 700 miles – but not if you unleash the entire 1,287 hp through all six electric motors!

Techrules plans to make just 10 of the astonishing Giugiaro-designed machines, and they will be available as single-, two- or three-seaters. In the three-seater, the passengers will sit either side of the driver, as in the McLaren F1.

##  Performance

| | |
|---|---|
| Top speed | 199 mph |
| 0–62 mph | 2.5 secs |
| Power | 1,287 hp |
| Torque | 7,800 Nm |

## Engine

| | |
|---|---|
| Capacity | 6 electric motors |
| Type | Turbine range extender |

##  Efficiency

| | |
|---|---|
| Mileage | 31.5 mpg |

##  Dimensions

| | |
|---|---|
| Kerb weight | 1,630 kg |
| Power/weight | 790 hp/tonne |
| Length | 4,694 mm |

# Glickenhaus SCG003S

**Country of manufacture** | **United States**

Jim Glickenhaus is an American car collector with a passion: to make his own race car that can match Europe's best. Now he has made a name for himself in endurance racing, he is converting his racer into a street machine that you can drive to the shops. You'll stop traffic, but there'll be nowhere to put the groceries.

The SCG003S – S for stradale or street version – has evolved from the competition car. In road legal trim it makes few concessions, but there are more mod cons in the enticing-looking cockpit.

 **Performance**

| | |
|---|---|
| Top speed | 217 mph |
| 0–62 mph | 3.0 secs |
| Power | 750 hp |
| Torque | 800 Nm |

 **Engine**

| | |
|---|---|
| Capacity | 4.4-litre V8 |
| Type | Twin turbocharged |

 **Efficiency**

| | |
|---|---|
| Mileage | Not available |

 **Dimensions**

| | |
|---|---|
| Kerb weight | 1,300 kg |
| Power/weight | 577 hp/tonne |
| Length | 4,810 mm |

# Vanda Dendrobium

**Country of manufacture** | **Singapore**

How's this for flower power? Unveiled at the Geneva Motor Show in 2017, the electric Dendrobium is named after a type of orchid, and the way its doors and roof open mimics the blossoming petals. It makes for a simply stunning machine, slated for production in 2020 so not all details are yet known.

The Dendrobium prototype, which was built by the UK's Williams Advanced Engineering company, features six-sided honeycomb-like buttons on the dash and even the air vents, front grille and headlight bezels repeat this motif.

 **Performance**

| | |
|---|---|
| Top speed | 200 mph |
| 0–62 mph | 2.7 secs (targeted) |
| Power | 1,000 hp |
| Torque | Not available |

 **Engine**

| | |
|---|---|
| Capacity | 90–100 kWh |
| Type | Electric motors |

 **Efficiency**

| | |
|---|---|
| Mileage | Not available |

 **Dimensions**

| | |
|---|---|
| Curb weight | 1,750 kg (targeted) |
| Power/weight | 571 hp/tonne (estimate) |
| Length | 5,540 mm |

**NIO EP9**

# NextEV NIO EP9

| Country of manufacture | China |
| --- | --- |

For a few weeks in 2017 the fastest road-registerable car at the Nürburgring Nordschleife ('Green Hell') was electric. A megawatt of power (1,342 hp) means lots of batteries and hefty weight, but with massive torque from zero revs and ace handling this poster car of the all-electric market is an absolute scorcher!

Ten EP9s are being made at US$1.48 million each. A high price tag, but then this car's carbon cockpit and chassis are designed to handle the physical demands of cornering at 3g! A jet fighter, for comparison, pulls 9g in vertical flight.

## Performance

| | |
| --- | --- |
| Top speed | 194 mph |
| 0–60 mph | 2.7 secs |
| Power | 1,342 hp |
| Torque | Not available |

## Engine

| | |
| --- | --- |
| Capacity | 4 electric motors |
| Type | Plug-in electric |

## Efficiency

| | |
| --- | --- |
| Mileage | Not available |

## Dimensions

| | |
| --- | --- |
| Kerb weight | 1,735 kg |
| Power/weight | 773 hp/tonne |
| Length | 4,888 mm |

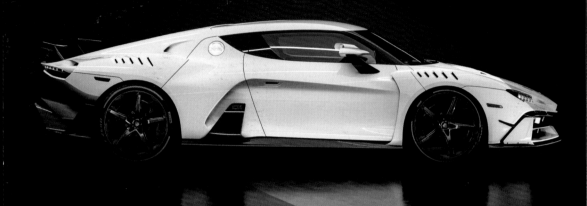

# ItalDesign Zerouno

**Country of manufacture** | **Italy**

ItalDesign has designed some of the most successful cars in history, like the VW Golf, but never made one of its own – until now. Zerouno (No. 01) is good looking, expensive and exclusive – just five are being made – and it's certainly fast. That's thanks to the V10 drivetrain from the Audi R8 behind the seats.

The Zerouno's interior is dominated by hand crafted carbon fibre. On the outside, meanwhile, racing stripes in the colours of the Italian flag run from nose to tail via the roof!

## Performance

| | |
|---|---|
| Top speed | 205 mph |
| 0–62 mph | 3.2 secs |
| Power | 610 hp |
| Torque | 560 Nm |

## Engine

| | |
|---|---|
| Capacity | 5.2-litre V10 |
| Type | Naturally aspirated |

## Efficiency

| | |
|---|---|
| Mileage | Not available |

## Dimensions

| | |
|---|---|
| Kerb weight | Not available |
| Power/weight | Not available |
| Length | 4,847 mm |

# Aston Martin Valkyrie

**Country of manufacture** | **United Kingdom**

The Valkyrie is the brainchild of F1 designer Adrian Newey who, with Red Bull Racing and Aston Martin, is defining a new level of road car performance. With ground-effect aerodynamics and about 1,000 hp propelling just 1,000 kg, the hybrid V12 aims to match a Le Mans winner: with 0–200 mph in an incredible 10 seconds.

Race car style for the road: that rectangular steering wheel may even be detachable, like an F1 car's, to aid entry and exit. The driving position is feet-up, F1-style, while cameras replace rear view mirrors.

 **Performance**

| | |
|---|---|
| Top speed | 250 mph (estimate) |
| 0–62 mph | 2.0 (estimate) |
| Power | 1,130 hp (estimate) |
| Torque | Not available |

 **Engine**

| | |
|---|---|
| Capacity | 6.5-litre V12 |
| Type | Petrol/electric hybrid |

 **Efficiency**

| | |
|---|---|
| Mileage | Not available |

 **Dimensions**

| | |
|---|---|
| Kerb weight | 1,130 kg (estimate) |
| Power/weight | 1,000 hp/tonne (estimate) |
| Length | Not available |

# Glossary

**0–60 mph/0–62 mph** – a standard test to measure, in seconds, how long a car takes to accelerate from zero to 60 mph (US) or 62 mph/100 kph (Europe).

## A

**acceleration** – a vehicle's capacity to gain speed.

**aerodynamic** – elements of a vehicle's shape that allows air to flow smoothly for less wind resistance.

**Alcantara** – durable man-made suede-like fabric.

**all-wheel drive (AWD)** – or 4x4, where power is transmitted to all four wheels.

## B

**biposto** – Italian for two-seater.

**biturbo** – *see twin turbocharged.*

**body** – panels covering the car's chassis and mechanical and electrical parts.

**bonnet** – or hood, this is a hinged cover over a car's engine.

**boxer engine** – or flat engine, where cylinders are horizontally-opposed either side of a crankshaft.

**Boxster** – used by Porsche for open top models with boxer engine and built on a roadster body.

**bumper** – a horizontal bar at front and/or back of a car to reduce collision damage.

## C

**carbon fibre** – a strong, lightweight carbon-fibre reinforced plastic.

**cabriolet (cabrio)** – a two-door car with a removable roof.

**chassis** – the base frame of a vehicle.

**concept car** – also prototype, one made to showcase new styling or technology.

**convertible** – a vehicle where a soft or hard roof can be opened and closed.

**coupe** – a sporty two-door car with a hard, fixed roof.

**crossover utility vehicle (CUV)** – a vehicle built on a car platform but with sport utility vehicle (SUV) features like high ground clearance.

**CVT** – continuously variable transmission.

**Cup** – model name that relates to a racing series.

**cylinder** – a chamber in an engine in which combustion takes place. Most cars have four-, six- or eight-cylinders arranged as flat/boxer (at 180° to each other), straight/inline (in a single row), V (angled away from each other) and double-V or W pattern.

## D

**diesel engine** – where air, compressed to a high temperature in the combustion chamber, ignites the diesel fuel.

**diffuser** – aerodynamic feature at the rear end of a car.

**downforce** – or ground effect, is aerodynamic design that increases vertical force and therefore grip.

**drivetrain** – components that generate power and transmit it to the wheels.

**dual-clutch** – automatic transmission with a clutch for even-numbered gears and one for odd-numbered gears.

## E

**efficiency** – how far a car will travel on a unit (imperial gallon) of fuel.

**electric vehicle (EV)** – uses energy stored in rechargeable batteries to drive electric motors.

**electronic stability system** – computerized technology to improve a car's traction.

**engine** – where chemical energy in a fuel is converted to mechanical energy in order to turn a shaft.

**engine size (capacity)** – measured in litres or cubic inches or centimetres (cu in or cc), it is the volume of air sucked in by all the pistons as they move from top to bottom of the cylinders.

**estate** – a large car with rear opening into a luggage/storage area.

**exhaust** – piping that carries the gases produced during combustion to the rear of the car.

## F

**factory tuned** – a model that has engine or chassis upgrades done by the manufacturer. Often indicated in the model name, like Mercedes-AMG, BMW M or Cadillac V-series.

**flat engine** – *see boxer engine.*

**front-wheel drive** – where power is directed only to the front wheels.

**four-wheel drive (4WD)** – *see all-wheel drive.*

## G

**gearbox** – or transmission or 'box, a metal box containing toothed cogs that are engaged manually, via a clutch and gear selector, or automatically to increase or decrease speed.

**grille** – an opening at the front of a car so air can pass to the radiator.

**GT** – Grand Touring or Gran Turismo; a high performance car.

**GTB** – Grand Tourer Berlinetta; a coupe-style GT.

**GTI (GTi)** – Grand Tourer Injection; a car with a fuel-injected engine.

**GTR (GT-R)** – Gran Turismo Racing

**GTS** – Gran Turismo Spider (convertible), Sport (four-door sedan) or Special.

## H

**handling** – how a vehicle steers and its manoeuvrability on corners.

**hatchback (hatch)** – a car with a full-width opening at the rear.

**horsepower (hp)** – the unit of measurement for engine power. Originally used to express the power of a steam locomotive in terms of the strength of draught horses.

**HSV** – Holden Special Vehicles

**hybrid** – a vehicle that has a battery-powered electric motor and a fuel-powered engine.

## K

**kerb weight** – total vehicle weight including fuel, fluids and standard equipment but no passengers or load.

**kilowatt hour (kWh)** – measure of the electric energy produced (or consumed) in an hour.

## L

**LED** – light-emitting diode.

**Le Mans** – 24-hour endurance car race held in Le Mans, France.

**length** – measured in millimetres (mm) from the most forward-facing point of a car to its most rear-facing point.

**LS** – Luxury Sedan.

## M

**marque** – another word for 'make of car'.

**megacar** – a car that has more than one megawatt (mW) or 1,340 hp of power.

**mileage** – or consumption or fuel economy, the distance a vehicle can travel on one unit of fuel. Tests to measure this vary between countries, but cover highway or city driving. A combined figure covers highway and city conditions. For all-electric cars, the mpg is a combustion engine equivalent.

**miles per gallon (mpg)** – miles travelled on an imperial gallon of fuel.

**muscle car** – American and Australian term for a high-performance car.

**N**

**naturally aspirated** – when air intake into the engine is determined only by atmospheric pressure.

**Newton metre (Nm)** – a measurement of force, where one Newton is the force required to accelerate a one-kilogram object one meter per second per second.

**NSX** – New Sportscar eXperimental.

**Nürburgring** – an old car race track in Germany. Nordschleife (known as 'Green Hell'), the north circuit, is now used mainly by manufacturers which test their powerful models there and aim to set the fastest lap times.

**O**

**oversteer** – when the rear tyres skid and the car turns into a corner more than the amount intended.

**P-Q**

**paddle shift** – *see semi-automatic transmission.*

**petrol (gasoline) engine** – fuel is ignited by a spark in the combustion chamber.

**pillar** – vertical or near vertical supports on a car, for example: A-pillars are either side of the windscreen; B-pillars, behind the front doors; C-pillars, behind the rear doors.

**piston** – a component that moves up and down inside a cylinder.

**power** – *see horsepower.*

**power to weight (hp/tonne)** – correlation between the power (hp) of an engine to the car's kerb weight (tonne).

**production car** – a mass-produced car on sale to the public and road legal.

**quattro** – Italian for four, and meaning four-wheel drive (Audi) or four-door (Maserati).

**R**

**R** – may indicate Race specification in a car's model name.

**RA** – Race Applicant.

**redline** – a red line on a car's rev counter (tachometer) that indicates maximum engine speed expressed as revolutions per minute.

**revolutions per minute (rpm)** – how many times per minute engine components, like the crankshaft, rotate.

**roadster** – a two-seater car with a folding roof.

**RS** – Rally Sport or Racing Sport.

**S**

**sedan** – or saloon, a medium to large fixed-roof, four-door car.

**semi-automatic transmission (SAT)** – gearbox where gears are chosen manually, but the clutch is automatic

**sequential gearbox** – a manual transmission where gears are selected by clicking a button, not moving a gear stick. Common on race cars.

**SL** – Sports Light or Series Limited.

**speed** – the rate at which a car moves, and also refers to the number of forward gear ratios, as in five- or six-speed, in the gearbox.

**speed limiter** – a device that limits a car's top speed. Some manufacturers, mostly European, limit their fastest models to 155 mph (250 kph).

**spider (spyder)** – a car with a removable roof.

**splitter** – aerodynamic feature at the front of the car.

**spoiler** – aerodynamic device to increase downforce by 'spoiling' the airflow over the car.

**sportback** – four-door hatchback where the roof starts sloping from behind the driver's door.

**sports car** – a small, powerful two-seater car.

**SRT** – Street & Racing Technology (Fiat Chrysler).

**ST** - Sports Technologies (Ford).

**stradale** – Italian for 'road-going', and usually indicates a road legal version of a track car.

**straight or inline** – *see cylinder.*

**supercharger** – an engine driven device that forcibly compresses air into the cylinders to increase power.

**suspension** – springs, dampers and anti-sway bars that maximize friction between tyres and road for handling, steering and comfort.

**Sport Utility Vehicle (SUV)** – a high-riding vehicle with a large opening at the rear.

**SV** – Special Version.

**switchgear** – the switches and electric controls in a car.

**T**

**targa** – a semi-convertible car where a section of roof can be removed.

**throttle** – another name for the accelerator pedal, and also for the system that controls the volume of air entering the engine.

**trim** – the materials, like wood, leather or metals, used to cover or decorate the interior of a car.

**torque** – the force generated by an engine to rotate the crankshaft at a given speed.

**transmission** – *see gearbox.*

**turbocharger** – an exhaust-gas driven turbine (fan) that forces air into the engine to increase power.

**twin turbocharged** – or biturbo, a car with two turbochargers.

**U-W**

**understeer** – when the front tyres skid and the car turns into a corner less than the amount intended.

**V** – this indicates an engine where the cylinders are arranged in a V-shape either side of the crankshaft.

**valves per cylinder** – the number of intake and exhaust valves in a cylinder.

**venturi** – an aerodynamic effect underneath a car.

**VXR** – race track-styled road car with high performance (Vauxhall).

**W** – an engine where cylinders are in banks resembling the letter W. For example, W16 with 16 cylinders.

# Index